Alternatives to Neoliberal Peacebuilding and Statebuilding in Africa

This book critically interrogates the neoliberal peacebuilding and statebuilding model and proposes a popular progressive model centred around the lived realities of African societies.

The neoliberal interventionist model assumed prominence and universal hegemony following the demise of state socialism at the end of the Cold War. However, this book argues that it is a primarily short-term, top-down approach that imposes Western norms and values on conflict and post-conflict societies. By contrast, the popular progressive model espoused by this book is based on stringent examination and analysis of the reality of the socio-economic development, structures, institutions, politics and cultures of developing societies. In doing so, it combines bottom-up and top-down, popular and elite, and long-term evolutionary processes of societal construction as a requisite for enduring peacebuilding and statebuilding.

By comparing and contrasting the dominant neoliberal peacebuilding and statebuilding model with a popular progressive model, the book seeks to empower locals (both elites and masses) to sit in the driver's seat and construct their own societies. As such, it is an important contribution to scholars, activists, policymakers, civil society organisations, NGOs and all those who are concerned with peace, stability and development across Africa and other developing countries.

Redie Bereketeab is Associate Professor of Sociology and Senior Researcher at The Nordic African Institute, Uppsala, Sweden.

Routledge Studies in African Development

African Peacekeeping Training Centres
Socialisation as a Tool for Peace?
Anne Flaspöler

Corporate Governance in Tanzania
Ethics and Accountability at the Crossroads
Peter C. Mhando

Economic Dualism in Zimbabwe
From Colonial Rhodesia to Post-Independence
Daniel B. Ndlela

Rethinking Ownership of Development in Africa
T.D Harper-Shipman

African Environmental Crisis
A History of Science for Development
Gufu Oba

Development in Nigeria
Promise on Hold?
Edlyne Eze Anugwom

Mineral Resource Governance and Human Development in Ghana
Felix Danso

Alternatives to Neoliberal Peacebuilding and Statebuilding in Africa
Redie Bereketeab

For more information about this series, please visit: https://www.routledge.com

Alternatives to Neoliberal Peacebuilding and Statebuilding in Africa

Redie Bereketeab

Routledge
Taylor & Francis Group

LONDON AND NEW YORK

First published 2021
by Routledge
2 Park Square, Milton Park, Abingdon, Oxon OX14 4RN

and by Routledge
52 Vanderbilt Avenue, New York, NY 10017

Routledge is an imprint of the Taylor & Francis Group, an informa business

British Library Cataloguing-in-Publication Data
A catalogue record for this book is available from the British Library

Library of Congress Cataloging-in-Publication Data
Names: Bereketeab, Redie, author.
Title: Alternatives to neoliberal peacebuilding and
statebuilding in Africa / Redie Bereketeab.
Other titles: Routledge studies in African development.
Description: Abingdon, Oxon; New York, N.Y.: Routledge, 2021. |
Series: Routledge studies in African development |
Includes bibliographical references and index.
Identifiers: LCCN 2020019679 (print) | LCCN 2020019680
(ebook) | ISBN 9780367558949 (hardback) |
ISBN 9781003095613 (ebook)
Subjects: LCSH: Peace-building—Africa. | Nation-building—Africa. |
Economic development—Africa. | Self-determination, National—Africa.
Classification: LCC JZ5584.A35 (print) |
LCC JZ5584.A35 (ebook) | DDC 327.172096—dc23
LC record available at https://lccn.loc.gov/2020019679
LC ebook record available at https://lccn.loc.gov/2020019680

ISBN: 978-0-367-55894-9 (hbk)
ISBN: 978-0-367-55896-3 (pbk)
ISBN: 978-1-003-09561-3 (ebk)

Typeset in Times New Roman
by codeMantra

Contents

1 Introduction

Understanding peacebuilding and statebuilding in the era of neoliberalism

Introduction

Making sense of peacebuilding and statebuilding (PBSB) is a great challenge of our time – a time characterised by the omnipresent, yet contested, reign of neoliberalism; a time also characterised by state fragility, crisis, failure and collapse; by terrorism, fundamentalism, extremism and interventionism affecting primarily the global south. The challenge gains additional currency when viewed from the vantage point of the peacebuilding–statebuilding nexus. Following the end of the Cold War – which also heralded the collapse of the Soviet-led Eastern bloc and state socialism – there was a need to change gear, in order to reconfigure world power and international relations. The reconfiguration spawned the phenomenon that came to be known as the New World Order, indicating the emergence of a hegemonic mono-polar politico-economic global order that was enthusiastically welcomed by the high priests of neoliberalism, such as Francis Fukuyama (1992) and Samuel P. Huntington (1996). This mono-polarity of the politico-economic order was celebrated as the triumph of the West over the East in the ideological struggle, and warranted the declaration of the 'end of history' (Paris, 2010). The triumphalist exhilaration was due to the perception that the West had secured hegemonic world domination. The consequence of the triumphalism, however, became a highly unstable world order.

This chapter seeks to understand PBSB in the era of neoliberalism. The neoliberal era that became dominant following the end of the Cold War and the collapse of state socialism is also characterised by extensive interventionism of big powers, primarily Western in the internal affairs of fragile, non-Western societies. This interventionism was driven by at least three interwoven phenomena. First, although many conflicts were resolved in the wake of the Cold War, many new ones broke out; these went on to engender fragility, failure and even the collapse of many states. Secondly, as a consequence, the failed states were labelled a danger to their own people and the wider world. In addition, they were perceived as fertile ground for the gestation of extremism, fundamentalism and terrorism. The rise of terrorism was, in turn, seen as a threat to Western security and interests, and particularly to those of the USA. Thirdly, the danger and threat perception induced two associated doctrines. One was the need to intervene to repair the failed states that are the sources of danger and threat. This led to the principle of humanitarian intervention in the cause of PBSB under the neoliberal regime. The other doctrine that emerged was that of pre-emptive action wherever the USA deemed it justifiable – and felt itself entitled – to attack an imagined 'enemy' state before it attacked the USA (Murphy, 2005; Peilouw et al., 2015; Thiessen, 2011).

Such interventionism represents a violation of international law and the sovereignty of weaker states, particularly when it takes place without a UN resolution. Indeed, many of the acts of interference in the internal affairs of states have been unprecedented and constitute a breach of the Treaty of Westphalia of 1648, which to this day governs inter-state relations. They also breach the UN Charter. The Treaty of Westphalia is based on the principle of the equality of states, regardless of their size and power; it gives protection against interference, invasion and threat, particularly from powerful states. The invasions of Iraq, Libya, Somalia and Democratic Republic of Congo (DRC), and the blunders in Syria, Mali and Yemen were all in blatant breach of UN and international law.

This book explores two models of PBSB. The first is associated with the neoliberal interventionist model, which, broadly speaking, deals with short-term PBSB in the wake of a devastating war. The second is concerned with long-term PBSB and relates to the gradual construction of socio-economic and political institutions in societies. The second model is termed 'popular progressive peacebuilding and statebuilding'. The two models succinctly attempt to analyse the challenges conflict and post-conflict developing societies face. In this respect, the scope of the book is to capture cases throughout the developing world. The aim of this chapter is briefly to introduce the two models. Those models are then fleshed out in detail in the remainder of the chapters.

The contention underpinning the analysis is that the two models of PBSB – popular progressive and neoliberal – are opposites. Popular progressive peacebuilding is historical, contemporary and futuristic.[1] Given this trajectory and evolution, there is a continuous time horizon connecting the past, the present and the future. The short-term interventionist neoliberal approach to PBSB – a theoretical and empirical notion that assumed prominence following the end of the Cold War (Call and Wyeth, 2008; Curtis and Dzinesa, 2012; Harrison, 2010) is time bound. As such, it cannot deal with the profound root causes of conflicts and wars, which by their very nature concern so-cietal construction. The reason for the growing prominence of PBSB is invariably related to the rise of neoliberal interventionist ideology, which replaced the Cold War order (Harrison, 2010), and to the crisis of the state in developing societies. The triumphalist neoliberal cause embarked on a proselytising mission of moulding humanity with ne-oliberal values and norms. Western values and norms were elevated to universal values and norms, after which every member of human-ity should strive (Tom, 2017). This proselytising drive has propelled an aggressive, interventionist approach to PBSB. Peacebuilding and statebuilding that did not follow neoliberal ideology were perceived not only as untenable, but also as a danger to world peace (Hutchful, 2012: 81; Zaum, 2012: 47).

Western interventionist PBSB offered an excellent opportunity to re-configure societies under stress into neoliberal societies, along Western lines. Referring to this, Roland Paris (2002: 638) notes: 'Without excep-tion, peacebuilding missions in the post-Cold War period have attempted to "transplant" the values and institutions of the liberal democratic core into the domestic affairs of peripheral host states.' He also designates it *mission civilisatrice* – a reminder of the European imperial powers' duty to colonise dependent populations in order to civilise them. Iraq, Afghanistan, Somalia, Libya, Sierra Leone, Central African Republic (CAR), DRC and South Sudan became guinea pigs for the newly dom-inant neoliberal PBSB interventionist doctrine (Call and Wyeth, 2008; Eriksen, 2009; Nhema and Zeleza, 2008; Paffenholz, 2015; Tom, 2017; Zambakari, 2016). The source of the stress of these fragile societies was viewed as an inadequate dose of the 'universal' values and norms. The remedy for the dysfunctionality of fragile societies was therefore as-sumed to be international intervention, with the intention of restructur-ing and rebuilding post-conflict countries along the lines of neoliberal values and norms – that is, providing a bigger dose of 'universal' values and norms.

Critics, however, argue that neoliberal PBSB is unsustainable and dysfunctional, as it is an external imposition and fails to take account of the specific realities and contexts of the particular society: social, cul-tural, historical, economic, political, structural, institutional and ethnic (Harrison, 2010; Lederach, 1997; Mac Ginty, 2008; Paffenholz, 2015).

Functional and sustainable PBSB needs to rely on the culture, history, social and political structures and forces of the society in question (Tom, 2017). It should draw on proven domestic institutions, mechanisms and authorities (Richmond, 2011). This is the underlying conception of the popular progressive model promoted in this book.

This chapter consists of six sections. The next section provides a broad overview of PBSB discourse. That is followed by an analysis of the conceptual framework. Then comes a discussion of the methodological framework. The next section provides the themes and organisation of the book. Finally, there are some concluding thoughts about how to deepen sustainable PBSB in Africa.

Peacebuilding and statebuilding: a broad overview

The project of PBSB is enduring and gradual. It is a long-term process (Maiese, 2003), not a one-time shot that sticks forever. Therefore, it needs continuous maintenance, refurbishment and innovation. The French historian Ernest Renan, in his classical piece of 1882a entitled 'What is a Nation?', called this phenomenon a daily plebiscite (Renan, 1991). That means it needs to be cultured, cultivated, fertilised, watered and nourished daily, in order to persistently and steadily grow healthy, strong and functional. PBSB as a general societal construction, like the nation not only demands constant attention but also perpetual renewal of the social contract that reinforces its perennial legitimacy in the eyes of citizens. In Renan's own words,

> A nation's existence is, if you will pardon the metaphor, a daily plebiscite, just as an individual's existence is a perpetual affirmation of life. That, I know full well, is less metaphysical than divine right and less brutal than so-called historical right. According to the ideas that I am outlining to you, a nation has no more right than a king does to say to a province: 'You belong to me, I am seizing you.' A province, as far as I am concerned, is its inhabitants; if anyone has the right to be consulted in such an affair, it is the inhabitant. A nation never has any real interest in annexing or holding on to a country against its will. The wish of nations is, all in all, the sole legitimate criterion, the one to which one must always return.
>
> (Renan, 1882b: 4)

PBSB is also intimately and dialectically connected with culture; history; socio-economic structures, institutions and traditions; authority of the particular society; moral and ethical imperatives. It is about integration, cohesion, developing commonalities and peaceful coexistence within a limited territory, under the umbrella of a common state. It rests on continuous and relentless hard work, preservation, innovation and lifetime caring. Boutros Boutros-Ghali defined peacebuilding as 'action to identify and support structures which will tend to strengthen and solidify peace in order to avoid relapse into conflict' (quoted in Barnett, 2006: 87).[2] In other words, it depends on the continuous and watchful attention of those who gain or lose from its decline or absence. The discourse of PBSB continues to engage and intrigue scholars, policymakers, activists, religious leaders and common citizens. Yet, discursive engagement is, most of the time, marked by radically diverging opinions; theoretical and ideological persuasions; epistemic, ontological and methodological controversies; and empirical strategies, policies and tactics. All this renders the field of PBSB a highly contested one both discursively and empirically.

At least four general theoretical conceptualisations of peacebuilding run through the mainstream literature: (i) structural violence theory, (ii) transformation relationship theory, (iii) protracted social conflict theory and (iv) relationship building (conflict resolution) theory (Paffenholz, 2015: 859). Peacebuilding is often defined as 'efforts at national, local, or international levels to consolidate peace in war-torn societies' (Call, 2008: 6). Statebuilding is also construed as a necessary requirement for peacebuilding. In this perception, a fully developed and functioning state arguably provides the infrastructures that underpin peace and peacebuilding. Ultimately, durable peacebuilding is concerned with the development of the will to live together, based on shared overarching values, interests, emotions and cognitions, mutual acceptance and recognition, cooperative interaction, common security, complementarity, institutionalisation of mechanisms for problem solving, widely shared goals and expectations (Gawerc, 2006: 442). These distinct properties gain extra validity in poly-ethnic, poly-glottic, poly-cultural and poly-religious societies. In other words, they are concerned with the protracted process and project of state- and nation-building (Mazrui and Wiafe-Amoako, 2016; Zaum, 2012). This conceptualisation of PBSB runs along the line of the progressive and popular conception suggested in this book.

Counter to the popular progressive notion of PBSB runs the neoliberal notion or ideology. Neoliberal ideology was popularised following the end of the Cold War and the collapse of state socialism, when post-Westphalian neoliberalist discourse and practice began to assume prominence (Hameiri, 2014; Tutuianu, 2013). For some, it was the demise of Keynesianism that paved the way for neoliberalism: 'One school of thought, common to those of an idealist disposition, views the shift from the Keynesian to the neoliberal era largely as the victory of one ideology over another' (Mitchell and Fazi, 2017: 36). Post-Keynesianism coincided with the post-Cold War era, which brought a double shift of absolute Western economic and political neoliberalism. Neoliberal hegemonic narrative and discourse embarked on the mission of reconfiguring the world order in the image of Western societies, and neoliberal high priests declared the 'end of history' (Fukuyama, 1992) and the 'clash of civilisations' (Huntington, 1996). The Hegelian notion of linear history is that it reaches its zenith with the final construction of the perfect state and is propelled by the struggle of opposites. Fukuyama's claim, therefore, was informed by his conviction that history had been driven by the struggle between liberal democracy and communism; and with the demise of the Soviet Union and state socialism, the triumph of one world order had been secured. For Huntington, on the other hand, the struggle of the political and ideological would be replaced by the struggle of civilisations, with a clash between Western civilisation and Islam. Neoconservatives in the USA took this literally in the wake of the 11 September 2001 terrorist attacks on the USA, and declared war on Islam.

Post-Cold War and post-conflict neoliberal interventionist PBSB has attempted to shape and reshape African societies in the Western mould of societal formation. The contemporary global order is to be refashioned along Western lines (Andrieu, 2010; Badie, 2000). Instead of bringing peace, however, this neoliberal conception has produced more conflicts and greater instability (Call, 2008; Call and Wyeth, 2008; Harrison, 2010; Steinberg, 2012; Tom, 2017). The reason for the failure of the endeavour to rebuild post-conflict African societies along neoliberal lines could be explained by the fact that it disconnects societies from their historical and social foundations and is one dimensional – an elitist, top-down strategy. It widens the gap between rural and urban, the elite and the masses, etc. Like a toppled tree, struggling to grow again with its roots exposed, post-conflict societies that are disconnected from their foundations also find it hard to build peace and stability. In this context, connecting to one's roots is a *sine qua non* for peace, stability and development (Davidson, 1992; Ekeh, 1983; Mazrui and Wiafe-Amoako, 2016). Therefore, the epistemological proposition here – an alternative model based on the idiosyncratic specificities of societies in Africa – is a prerequisite for durable PBSB. This might sound anachronistic in an era of globalisation. Note should be taken, however, that 'globalization is increasingly becoming more synonymous with re-colonization' (Shittu, 2015: 44). Globalisation as an international mechanism based on neoliberal ideology is increasingly looking like a jail, where some people (the prison guards) have full rights and freedoms and other people (the prisoners) have no rights and no freedom whatsoever. This is so because globalisation is not constructed on a level playing field. It is dictated by hierarchically arranged power structures and relations (Carmody and Owusu, 2018: 63). Indeed, the structure defining globalisation is pyramidal, with a few privileged perched on the apex, but the overwhelming majority squeezed in at the base. The power structures and relations are reinforced by capital, whose playground is the market, which is designed to benefit the affluent and powerful. Moreover, neoliberal globalisation, dictated by principles of market economy and capital, disarms and undermines progressive national developmental forces through measures of 'delocalisation, deindustrialisation, the free movement of goods and capital, etc.' (Mitchell and Fazi, 2017: 7).

> 'Globalization' is the establishment of an international system tending toward unification of its rule, values, and objectives, while claiming to integrate within its center the whole of humanity ... by stimulating the importation of Western models into societies in the South, it reveals its inadequacy; by inciting peripheral societies to adapt, it raises hope of innovation that may very well be false; by rushing the process of world unification, it encourages the rebirth and affirmation of individual characteristics; by endowing the international order with a center of power more structured than ever, it tends to intensify conflict. By seeking to bring historical development to an end, it suddenly launches History in varied and contradictory directions.
>
> (Badie, 2000: 1–2)

Peacebuilding is more than the absence of war (known as negative peace) (Gawerc, 2006; Oda, 2007). It presupposes the elimination of cultural, social, political, economic, structural and institutional violence. Positive peacebuilding is concerned with multidimensional non-war-related social issues, such as the provision of services, equitable distribution of resources, development, building ethnic relations, poverty alleviation. The right to education and health, mutual respect and recognition are further dimensions of positive peacebuilding (Curtis, 2012; Maiese, 2003). Positive peace is a step on from negative peace: that is, if negative peace constitutes the *necessary* conditions, then positive peace constitutes the *sufficient* conditions for functional and sustainable peace and peacebuilding (Galtung, 1967). The fulfilment of the necessary and sufficient conditions for PBSB demands concerted efforts on the part of all societal groups. It is a product of structural and systematic negotiations, bargains, compromises, conciliation and dialogue among stakeholders.

The Westphalian order, with its basic tenets of respect for national sovereignty, territorial integrity and non-interference, brought relative peace and stability to the state world system (Osiander, 2001; Teschke, 2002; Watson, 1990). The Treaty of Westphalia was a systemic attempt to address chaotic, unregulated and barbaric inter-state relations. The post-Cold War order that disrupted the Westphalian order (based as it was on non-interference), spurred uncertainty, disorder, inequality, social rupture, conflict and war, as evidenced in Afghanistan, Iraq, Libya, Syria, Yemen and Somalia (Cordesman, 2016; Held and Ulrichsen, 2011; Thiessen, 2011). In the post-Cold War and post-Westphalia world, where state sovereignty, non-interference and territorial integrity are successively and systematically being eroded, 'there are indications of gradual shift away from purely horizontal, and thus intergovernmental or Westphalian, to more vertical, and thus supranational or post-Westphalian, structure of the global order' (Kreuder-Sonnen and Zangl, 2014: 570). The new world order that induced Western hegemony has so far proven to be a recipe for intrusion, conflict, war and instability. The defining characteristics of the new world order have been chaos and anarchy, induced by disequilibrium in global humanity; as a result of this, domination by a certain section of global humanity – as implied by mono-polarity – has become the overriding feature (Harrison, 2010).

Profound and sustainable peacebuilding requires going beyond administrative, technical and legal subscriptions, and endorsing the basic sociological dimension of the societal construction of state- and nation-building in Africa. It is through evolutionary (but not necessarily unilinear) protracted societal formation that durable and genuine peacebuilding can be achieved. It is also certain that this profound societal construction could not be undertaken by external intervention. Africa is in need of genuine domestic nation and state construction that ensures enduring peace and peacebuilding. This work is a contribution towards that objective.

Conceptual issues

A number of conceptual edifices are employed in this book. The central ones are liberalism/neoliberalism, PBSB. Here I flesh out my understanding of liberalism and neoliberalism; the others are dealt with in later chapters and sections. The peace and peacebuilding literature is permeated with several inter-related conceptual and theoretical terminologies. These include liberal peace, liberal peace thesis, liberal peace theory, peacekeeping, peace mediation, conflict resolution and prevention. My concern in this work is however, limited to neoliberal PBSB as an ideology bent to reconfigure non-Western conflict affected societies along Western mould. No matter how important the mentioned concepts may be in the literature of PBSB, I have made the option of not including them in this work. Harrison (2010) describes neoliberalism as an ideology and as global social engineering. He further purports 'neoliberalism which is driven by a set of interrelated agendas: to homogenise socio-cultural diversity, to project Western power throughout the world, to construct global market order and to reconfigure class relations in favour of property' (Harrison, 2010: 26). Following Harrison's notion of reconfiguring and 'as a global policy raft and political ideology' (Harrison, 2010: 18), I conceptualise neoliberalism in this work as an ideological exercise to reconfigure non-Western conflict affected societies along Western mould.

Here I would like to provide a succinct exposition of the related concepts of liberalism and neoliberalism. These are the two most difficult concepts to deal with. One reason for the difficulty is that they are an ideologically charged pair of concepts. They are also the most misunderstood and abused (perhaps intentionally) concepts. They mean different things to different people and can cover economic, political, ideological, cultural, social, geostrategic or historical aspects – or all of the above simultaneously. In addition, oftentimes, they are used interchangeably, contributing to further confusion. Let me make clear my position from the very outset. To me, liberalism and neoliberalism are two distinct concepts. I join those who perceive neoliberalism as an all-encompassing, ideologically charged concept used to reconfigure conflict-ridden and post-conflict non-Western societies along Western lines of norms and values. In this book, I use the concept of neoliberalism in a narrow sense, related to PBSB in conflict and post-conflict so-called 'fragile' societies or failed states. My interest is in its ideologically driven application.

The common-sense understanding makes little effort to distinguish between liberalism and neoliberalism. Indeed, there are those who think neoliberalism is another version of liberalism (Poku and Whitman, 2018). This might be a conscious, choreographed, intentional endeavour particularly by those who are ideologically motivated, or maybe an innocent lack of clear understanding. Right-wing and neo-conservative scholars conflate liberalism and neoliberalism, in order to dilute the ideological and doctrinal connotation of the latter.

The classical notion of liberalism related individual freedom, equality, brotherhood, etc. would make it tenable to accept neoliberalism. Nevertheless, the plethora of definitions and conceptualisations make neoliberalism highly contested, contradictory, vague and ambiguous, leading some to suggest that the concept has no useful scientific or analytical meaning (Lynch, 2017). In this work, however, a clear distinction is drawn between the two. Classical liberalism – with its emphasis on the trinity values of liberty, fraternity and equality – was widely perceived as the foundation stone of the political and social philosophy of humanism, as it evolved in the West. This individual-centred humanism, a product of the Enlightenment period, advocated the pre-eminence of the secularised, urbanised, modernised, atomised individual as the embodiment of freedom, against the collectivist philosophy that celebrates society. Collectivist versus individualist eventually constituted the philosophical and theoretical battleground in social sciences, framed in the libertarian versus communitarian discourse (Greenfeld, 1992). The philosophical struggle was billed as being between the atomic individual and collectivist society – although it became increasingly clear that the distinction was superficial, because society is an aggregation of individuals, and individuals could not have existence outside society. In spite of the superficiality of the dichotomy, however, the polarity continued to define philosophy and social theory. In addition, proponents of the dichotomy suggested that historically, over a period of time and space, the evolutionary transformation from a communitarian to a libertarian society led to a transition from a communitarian to a libertarian era, where we are today.

The process that brought the sociological transformation was aptly propounded by classical sociologists like Emile Durkheim, Auguste Comte, Herbert Spencer and Ferdinand Tönnies (Sztompka, 1993). Durkheim, for instance, talks of mechanical solidarity and organic solidarity in describing the transformation process (Durkheim, 1984). According to him, evolutionary processes brought a density and concentration of human settlement, fostering differentiation and specialisation that generated historical transformation from mechanical to organic solidarity. Others also talk of transformation from an agrarian society to an industrial and post-industrial society (Gellner, 1983). Therefore, there is a long tradition in Western philosophy and social theory on which neoliberalism can comfortably lean. Critical interrogation, however, would shake up this comfortable ground if neoliberalism is extended beyond its spatiotemporal application or the origin to Africa.

In spite of voices critical of its applicability outside its spatiotemporal origin (of which this work is one), neoliberalism is increasingly assuming hegemonic status and is becoming a catch-all concept (see Poku and Whitman, 2018). Echoing this perception, Clarke notes:

> Whether we treat neo-liberalism from the standpoint of capitalist regimes of accumulation, or as a version of liberal governmentality, most of its political work involves practices of de- and re-articulation: reorganizing principles, policies, practices, and discourses into new configurations, assemblages, or constellations.
>
> (quoted in Swatuk, 2018: 118)

It is this practice of de- and re-articulations, configurations, assemblages and constellations that particularly target non-Western societies what this work is criticising. The catch-all nature renders neoliberalism devoid of any meaningful substance (Little, 2008; Smith, 2008). Little (2008: 148), for instance, notes:

> The term 'neo-liberalism' increasingly lays claim to an enormous terrain of political, social, economic, and cultural phenomena often so loosely applied and defined that it seems to be lurking almost everywhere.

Understandably, the very foundation of neoliberalism's mushrooming is also incurring criticism from different directions:

> The 'neoliberal university' is less about the advancement of analytical understanding and circulation of ideas, transmitted as 'gift' of one epistemic community to another and to society as a whole. Instead, it is more like a centre of 'applied expertise and vocational training ... [that is subordinated] to a society's economic strategy'; thereby risking the devaluation of its time-honoured task of training for democratic and critical citizenship, encouraging critical thinking and defending academic freedom. This restructuring has created de-politicised and sanitised research, instead of more radical enquiries that for instance challenge the ways in which power is exercised and inequality (and more broadly social order) is maintained. In synthesis, the neoliberal university is a major site in the 'struggle between knowledge for its own sake and commodified learning'.
>
> (Wiegratz et al., 2018: 10)

Neoliberalism's fascination with individual rights, the centrality of property rights, the culture of individualism, consumption and market-based populism gave primacy to economic neoliberalism at the expense of its political counterpart (Thompson, 2005). This compact package of knowledge, rights, practices and consumerisms was developed to explain and analyse Western societies; its validity and applicability as a concept for non-Western societies and PBSB is at the centre of this work. It is as a critical response to this 'compact package' that I advance the concept of popular progressive PBSB that will be developed in later chapters and sections.

A very brief treatment of the other central concept of the book – which I have termed 'popular progressive' – is warranted for two reasons. First, to give readers a succinct sense of what I mean from the very outset. The connotation of 'popular' denotes its people-centred nature, unlike the elitist approach of neoliberalism. 'Popular' invites active, conscious and decisive participation, ownership, setting of agenda and agency of common people. The concept of 'progressive' indicates the long-term, continuous, past-present-future-oriented nature of PBSB. Moreover, it is an indication of the profound nature of PBSB that concerns the basic and fundamental issues of nation and state formation that is societal construction.

The second reason is that – unlike neoliberalism – the term 'popular progressive approach' does not feature widely in the literature as an alternative to neoliberal PBSB. In fact, so far as I am aware, no one has used the phrase before. A number of scholars who are more or less critical of neoliberal approaches have used different concepts, mostly in an attempt to reform neoliberal interventionist PBSB. These would include: institutionalisation before liberalisation (IBL) (Paris, 2004); republican peacebuilding (Barnett, 2006); local peacebuilding (Chandler, 2013; Mac Ginty, 2008; Lederach, 1997); indigenous, bottom-up (Reno, 2008; Richmond, 2011); emancipatory peacebuilding (Thiessen, 2011). Unlike the popular progressive, which aims at a radical overhaul of the approach to PBSB, these scholars aim to reform it, reconcile and bridge the gap between the local and the international. Some of them simply announce, 'International actors must serve as facilitators for elite-grassroots interaction' (Thiessen, 2011: 130). The position of the popular progressive is that facilitation is neither a necessary nor a sufficient condition for overhauling neoliberalism.

Methodological framework

PBSB conceptualised as societal construction – or in technical parlance, nation and state formation – is by its very nature a macro-sociological endeavour. As a macro-sociology level of analysis it is embedded in and embodies multi-level structures and a range of actors. The metamorphosis of structures and actors involved in the formation and transformation of nations and states occurs in space and time, which mature in historical trajectory in specific cultural, economic, social and political internal processes and interactions. These processes and interactions require relevant or corresponding methodological analysis, explanation, understanding and interpretation. If we fail to galvanise that methodological instrumentality we will certainly fail to understand PBSB. The interplay of actors, structures, factors and relations makes it imperative to employ methodological pluralism. PBSB tuned to the macro-level may involve top-down approaches and strategies, at the same time as it also affects and involves local sub-national communities; the micro-sociological level would be involved with bottom-up approaches and strategies. In addition, the conflation of top-down and bottom-up strategies in the process of nation formation and state formation also reflects a double legacy. The double legacy represents an admixture of precolonial and colonial formations. A successful state formation and nation formation is understood here as a requisite for functional and enduring PBSB. In this vein then the popular progressive model of PBSB should necessarily concern itself with a combination of the macro- and the micro-levels; with a top-down and bottom-up methodological hybridity. This macro-level, micro-level, top-down, bottom-up methodological mix would cover what Peter Ekeh (1975) termed the two publics that were created by colonialism and that are very much alive and reflected in the conflicts afflicting post-colonial societies. The advantage of this kind of methodological framework is that PBSB as profoundly societal construction captures the multi-dimensional and multifaceted aspects of construction.

We are warned not to fall into the trap of comparison by the methodological analogy (Mamdani, 1996) that through analogical comparison with Western models denies the existence of certain properties that are inherently specific and belong to some societies and that should serve as a benchmark for evaluation, particularly in developing societies. Explaining this, Mamdani (2017: 9) notes: 'The residual or deviant case was understood not in terms of what it was, but with reference to what it was not. "Premodern" thus became "not yet modern", and "precapitalism" "not yet capitalism".' This is, further accentuated in the pot-Cold War era of neoliberal interventionist PBSB. Change or modernity needs to be conceptualised as inherent dynamism, instead of as a Western phenomenon that non-Western societies aspire to imitate or might be able to reach in the distant future, or are forced by external actors to adopt as part of the neoliberal social engineering PBSB. That particular version of modernity should not serve as a benchmark for how we perceive change in society. This certainly has implications for the validity of the methodological approach of the alternative popular progressive model.

Methodological individualism would aptly describe neoliberal PBSB, while methodological collectivism would describe popular progressive PBSB. Without subscribing to the Western model of development and modernity, which is based on 'industrialization, urbanization, rationalization, bureaucratization, democratization, the ascendency of capitalism, the spread of individualism and achievement motivation, the affirmation of reason and science' (Sztompka, 1993: 129), we should be able to interpret and analyse the transformation and modernisation of post-colonial societies drawing on methodological collectivism, which has relevance to societal construction – and thereby to PBSB. Methodological individualism (developed to analyse individual-centric societal formation) and methodological collectivism (developed to analyse collective-centric societal formation) are perceived as two methodological opposites dealing with neoliberalism and the popular progressive approach, respectively. While methodological individualism rests on ego-centrism, methodological collectivism rests on socio-centric. The main focus of the first is on PBSB that is top-down, elitist and foreign driven; while the second is an attempt at reconciling the top-down and bottom-up, the national–local and elite–mass approaches.

My critique of the interventionist neoliberal PBSB is directed towards the intentional and systematic attempt at reconfiguring conflict-affected fragile societies along the line of the Western model. As mentioned earlier, I am not interested in liberal peace, liberal peace theory, liberal peacekeeping, mediation, etc.; or liberalism in general. My choice of the alternative popular progressive model of PBSB is informed by the need of real, genuine and profound societal construction, meaning nation and state formation. Nation and state formation as understood in this work is a gradual, protracted, evolutionary and historical process that involves protracted negotiations, compromises, bargains among societal stakeholders, which in post-colonial societies is still work in progress. This leads me to assert societal construction of nation and state formation is a *sine qua non* for enduring PBSB. That leads me to a further assertion that interventionist neoliberal acts and actors could not achieve an enduring PBSB. Echoing this perception, Tom (2017: 2), for instance, notes, 'Post-conflict peacebuilding interventions have tended to result in 'no war, no peace' (Mac Ginty, 2008) or 'no peace, no war' (Richards, 2005a) situations in most post-conflict situations'. PBSB is, therefore, by its very nature domestic, political, gradual and transformative and involves multiple societal stakeholders, actors, structures, institutions and authorities. In short, the fundamentals of the project of PBSB are intimately connected with nation and state formation.

The methodology underpinning this work is qualitative text analysis: it draws on existing texts and scholarly works, and is informed by interpretative sociology. It attempts to interpret and understand the existing neoliberal literature and discourse of PBSB, on the one hand, and to construct a popular progressive discourse, on the other. In other words, involves methodologies of deconstruction (neoliberal PBSB) and construction (popular progressive PBSB). Hence, it is an attempt to advance a methodology of popular progressive literature and discourse of PBSB that is holistic and eclectic. The holistic and eclectic nature of the methodological approach is driven by the multi-disciplinary and plurality nature of the study. It navigates borders of various disciplines such as history, political science, sociology, conflict studies and international relations. History contributes to our understanding of trajectories and processes; political science would have a significant input in perception of power relations and distributions; sociology would aid us to understand societal construction: nation and state formation; while international relations may help us understand global relations and interventions.

Themes and organisation of the book

The central themes of the book are peacebuilding, statebuilding and linkage with neoliberalism and the popular progressive model. It concerns construction of an alternative model to neoliberal PBSB. It contends a functional and enduring peace and peacebuilding rests on profound societal construction: nation formation and state formation. It argues societal construction is a necessary requirement for lasting peace. Stemming from this contention the book offers a strong critique of the neoliberal PBSB model. The book aims to provide not just a reformist critique of the neoliberal model, but an alternative model. This alternative seeks to proffer innovative examination and analysis of PBSB. The alternative model is popular progressive PBSB, and is based on serious examination and analysis of non-Western societal reality, socio-economic development, structures, institutions, politics and cultures that are thought to be conducive to PBSB on the continent. The scope of the book is arranged in such a way that it serves to illustrate the problem of PBSB in conflict-stricken developing societies world over, without going deeper into a particular region. The overall objective of the book is to provide an outline and overview of the features of neoliberal PBSB and popular progressive PBSB. In recent years, there has been an explosion in the literature of neoliberal PBSB. Unfortunately, the literature of popular progressive PBSB is extremely scanty. Indeed, I could claim with confidence that this work is the only complete and exhaustive treatment of popular progressive PBSB. This makes it a novelty in the search for an alternative to neoliberalism in the area of PBSB. The book consists of six chapters.

This chapter has introduced the theme of the book and has provided an overview of the central concepts of PBSB employed in it. The next chapter, 'Neoliberal Peacebuilding and Statebuilding', analyses the neoliberal regime. Neoliberal interventionist PBSB has been pursued in conflict and post-conflict conditions of fragility, failure and collapse. The rationale for the intervention is always the perception that a failed state is a danger to its own people and to the world in general, and thus needs to be 'cured'. The chapter examines the process, mechanism and ideological motives of intervention. It argues that neoliberal PBSB is characterised by short-term, technical and administrative approaches, and is an elitist, top-down, external imposition. It analyses the three mechanisms by which Western values and norms acquire universality: socialisation, internalisation and externalisation. This is followed by an analysis of neoliberal peacebuilding that is followed by an analysis of neoliberal statebuilding. These two sections constitute the core of the chapter. The next section addresses state fragility. It argues why it is regarded as important to fix fragile and failed states. The chapter poses (and seeks to answer) the question of whether neoliberal interventionist PBSB can cure the pathologies afflicting fragile societies. The last section of the chapter provides some concluding thoughts.

Chapter 3, 'Popular Progressive Peacebuilding and Statebuilding', provides an alternative to neoliberal PBSB. It examines and analyses the conditions and features that characterise popular progressive PBSB as an alternative approach. The central objective of the popular progressive model is to interrogate the indigenous institutions, structures, authorities, mechanisms and dynamics deemed to uphold substantive PBSB. The popular progressive model contends that PBSB is concerned with fundamental societal construction – or, in technical parlance, with nation and state formation. It is therefore long-term, gradual and piecemeal work. The chapter contends PBSB is political by nature and has to do with power allocation. As such, it craves negotiation, bargaining and compromise by all stakeholders. It is also domestic by nature: it should thus be based on the subject of a society's culture, history, socio-economic level of development, etc. The chapter also navigates the notions of participatory democracy as a requirement of enduring PBSB, and ends with some concluding remarks.

Chapter 4, 'State Emancipation and Societal Pacification as Prerequisites for Peacebuilding', analyses the concepts of emancipation and pacification. It stresses that the emergence of state emancipation and societal pacification constitutes a necessary condition for sustainable and functional peace and peacebuilding. The chapter analyses peacebuilding in terms of state emancipation and societal pacification. State emancipation is concerned with developments whereby a state stands above societal groups and retains its autonomy; meanwhile, societal pacification refers to the sole right of the state to employ means of coercion, while society voluntarily abstains from possessing or using means of coercion. The emergence of these two phenomena indicates the full maturity of a state, indicating a relationship between state and society and the principles that govern that relationship. The rise of state emancipation and societal pacification is predicated on state penetration of society: a state incapable of penetrating society would not be able to bring about emancipation and pacification. This mutual development of state emancipation and societal pacification is informed by the sociological tradition that expounds the evolutionary historical transformation that leads to nation and state formation. It is also informed by the sociological assumption of checks and balances that regulate state–society relation, and that ultimately power emanates from the people. The chapter contends that state emancipation and societal pacification are products of the evolution over a considerable period of time of nation and state formation, which is dictated primarily by domestic reality. The final section of the chapter provides some concluding remarks.

Chapter 5, 'Statebuilding and Peacebuilding: Harmony and Discordance', analyses the relationship between statebuilding and peacebuilding. Some of the mainstream literature on statebuilding and peacebuilding maintains that harmony prevails between the two; other elements of the literature refute this. Much of the literature argues that they complement each other, or that one is the necessary condition for the other. This chapter, however, argues that discordance is rather the defining feature of the relationship. The basis for the discord is that statebuilding as a political project concerns power, and creates winners and losers – which is a source of conflict. The losers are certainly inclined to look for ways and means to address their grievances that might be far from peaceful. Peacebuilding, on the other hand, strives to bring together and reconcile all stakeholders and to forge peace among them. This presupposes the avoidance of classes of winners and losers. Therefore, at least initially, there is discord between *peacebuilding* and *statebuilding*. Moreover, the chapter contends, although, in the long run the two may converge, in the transitional period, however, divergence characterises the relationship. The chapter concludes that neoliberal PBSB is designed to foster discord between the two, unlike the popular progressive model, which aims at reconciling them. A final section of the chapter provides some concluding remarks.

Chapter 6, 'Conclusion: Summary and Highlights', provides summaries, highlights and the conclusions reached. The chapter reviews the central argument of the book, and its two main sections recap on neoliberal PBSB and popular progressive PBSB. It is the principal conclusion of the book that the popular progressive approach is superior to the neoliberal approach in ensuring functional and enduring PBSB. One section examines the consequences of neoliberal PBSB interventions: it contends that neoliberal-driven PBSB in post-conflict and conflict-developing societies plays a rather negative role, as is witnessed in countries such as Iraq, Syria, Libya, Somalia, South Sudan, Mali, DRC and CAR. Conversely, another section underscores that the popular progressive model creates harmony, unity, peace and development. The final section concludes that the two models of PBSB discussed in the book represent diametrically opposite approaches.

Conclusion

To recapitulate what has been discussed in this chapter, the book endeavours to examine neoliberal PBSB, on the one hand, and popular progressive PBSB, on the other. The central message of this chapter is that popular progressive PBSB is superior to neoliberal PBSB. This contention is examined in detail in the rest of the book. The superiority of the popular progressive model with regard to PBSB rests on two aspects. First, while neoliberal PBSB is short-term oriented, the popular progressive approach takes a long-term view. In addition, while the neoliberal approach is concerned with technical, administrative and external expertise-based solutions and approaches, the popular progressive model focuses on substantive, profound political and internal expertise-based solutions and approaches. The latter also depends overwhelmingly on indigenous institutions, mechanisms, structures and authorities. While it employs bottom-up and top-down strategies, neoliberal PBSB takes an elitist top-down approach. Secondly, while the neoliberal approach is bent on reconfiguring post-conflict fragile societies along the lines of Western norms, values and models, popular progressive PBSB regards the fundamentals of nation- and statebuilding as prerequisites for functional and sustainable PBSB. The neoliberal model addresses the symptoms of the problem rather than the basic roots. The diverging models and approaches framed in this chapter are examined and analysed in the following chapters.

Notes

1 What I have called here 'popular progressive peacebuilding' is usually referred to in the general literature as local (Chandler, 2013; Lederach, 1997; Mac Ginty, 2011), indigenous, bottom-up (Reno, 2008; Richmond, 2011). Michael Barnett (2006) distinguishes between liberal peacebuilding and republican peacebuilding, which is close to what I have called in this chapter popular progressive versus neoliberal. According to Barnett, while liberalism refers to the creation of a post-conflict state defined by rule of law, markets and democracy, republicanism refers to principles of deliberation, constitutionalism and representation that help a state recovering from war to foster stability and legitimacy. A legitimate state must be organised around liberal democratic principles (Barnett, 2006: 88–89).
2 Definitions abound in the literature of peacebuilding. This chapter is, however, not concerned with definitions of peacebuilding, but rather with the distinction between two theoretical strands identified here.

References

Andrieu, Koran. 2010. 'Civilising Peace-Building: Transitional Justice, Civil Society and the Liberal Paradigm', *Security Dialogue*, vol. 41, no. 5, pp. 537–558.
Badie, Bertrand. 2000. *The Imported State: The Westernization of the Political Order*. Stanford, CA: Stanford University Press.
Barnett, Michael. 2006. 'Building a Republican Peace: Stabilizing States after War', *International Security*, vol. 30, no. 4, pp. 87–112.
Call, Charles T. 2008. 'Ending Wars, Building States', in Charles T. Call and Vanessa Wyeth (eds.), *Building States to Build Peace*. Boulder, CO and London: Lynne Rienner Publishers, pp. 1–22.
Call, Charles T. and Wyeth, Vanessa (eds.). 2008. *Building States to Build Peace*. Boulder, CO and London: Lynne Rienner Publishers.
Carmody, Padraig and Owusu, Francis. 2018. 'Neoliberalism, Urbanization and Change in Africa', in Nana Poku and Jim Whitman (eds.), *Africa under Neoliberalism*. London and New York: Routledge, pp. 61–75.
Chandler, David. 2013. 'Peacebuilding and the Politics of Non-linearity: Rethinking "Hidden" Agency and "Resistance"', *Peacebuilding*, vol. 1, no. 1, pp. 17–32.
Cordesman, Anthony H. 2016. 'US Wars in Iraq, Syria, Libya and Yemen: What Are the Endstates?', Center for Strategic and International Studies. https://www.csis.org/analysis/us-wars-iraq-syria-libya-and-yemen-what-are-endstates

Curtis, Devon. 2012. 'The Contested Politics of Peacebuilding in Africa', in Devon Curtis and Gwinyayi Dzinesa (eds.), *Peacebuilding, Power, and Politics in Africa*. Athens: Ohio University Press, pp. 1–28.

Curtis, Devon and Dzinesa, Gwinyayi (eds.). 2012. *Peace-Building, Power, and Politics in Africa*. Athens: Ohio University Press.

Davidson, Basil. 1992. *The Black Man's Burden: Africa and the Curse of the Nation-State*. London: James Currey.

Durkheim, Emile. 1984. *The Division of Labour in Society*. London: Macmillan Press.

Ekeh, Peter P. 1983. *Colonialism and Social Structure: An Inaugural Lecture Delivered at the University of Ibadan on Thursday, 5 June 1980*. Nigeria: Ibadan University Press.

Ekeh, Peter P. 1975. 'Colonialism and the Two Publics in Africa: A Theoretical Statement', *Comparative Studies in Society and History*, vol. 17, no. 1, pp. 91–112.

Eriksen, Stein Sundstol. 2009. 'The Liberal Peace Is Neither: Peace-Building, State Building and the Reproduction of Conflict in the Democratic Republic of Congo', *International Peacekeeping*, vol. 16, no. 5, p. 666.

Fukuyama, Francis. 1992. *The End of History and the Last Man*. New York: Avon Books.

Galtung, Johan. 1967. *Theories of Peace: A Synthetic Approach to Peace Thinking*. Oslo: International Peace Research Institute.

Gawerc, Michelle I. 2006. 'Peacebuilding: Theoretical and Concrete Perspectives', *Peace and Change*, vol. 31, no. 4, pp. 435–478.

Gellner, Ernest. 1983. *Nations and Nationalism*. Oxford and Cambridge, MA: Blackwell Publishers.

Greenfeld, Liah. 1992. *Nationalism: Five Roads to Modernity*. Cambridge, MA and London: Harvard University Press.

Hameiri, Shahar. 2014. 'The Crisis of Liberal Peacebuilding and the Future of Statebuilding', *International Politics*, vol. 51, no. 3, pp. 316–333.

Harrison, Graham. 2010. *Neoliberal Africa: The Impact of Global Social Engineering*. London and New York: Zed Books.

Held, David and Ulrichsen, Kristian Coates. 2011. 'War of Decline: Afghanistan, Iraq and Libya', *Open Democracy*, 12 December.

Huntington, Samuel P. 1996. *The Clash of Civilizations and the Remaking of World Order*. New York: Touchstone.

Hutchful, Eboe. 2012. 'Security Sector Governance and Peace-Building', in Devon Curtis and Gwinyayi Dzinesa (eds.), *Peace-Building, Power, and Politics in Africa*. Athens: Ohio University Press, pp. 63–86.

Kreuder-Sonnen, Christian and Zangl, Bernhard. 2014. 'Which Post-Westphalia? International Organizations between Constitutionalism and Authoritarianism', *European Journal of International Relations*, vol. 2, no. 3, pp. 568–594.

Lederach, John Paul. 1997. *Building Peace: Sustainable Reconciliation in Divided Societies*. Washington, DC: United States Institute of Peace.

Little, Peter D. 2008. 'Comment: Reflection on Neo-Liberalism in Africa', *Focaal: European Journal of Anthropology*, vol. 51, pp. 148–150.

Lynch, Casey. 2017. '"Vote with Your Feet": Neoliberalism, the Democratic Nation-State, and Utopian Enclave Libertarianism', *Political Geography*, vol. 59, pp. 82–91.

Mac Ginty, Roger. 2011. 'Hybrid Peace: How Does Hybrid Peace Come About?', in Campbell, S., Mac Ginty, R., Chandler, D. and Sabaratnam, M. (eds.), *A Liberal Peace?: The Problems and Practices of Peacebuilding*. London: Zed Book, pp. 209–225.

Mac Ginty, Roger. 2008. 'Indigenous Peace-Making versus the Liberal Peace', *Coopeation and Conflict: Journal of the Nordic International Studies Association*, vol. 43, no. 2, pp. 139–163.

Maiese, Michelle. 2003. Peacebuilding. https://www.beyondintractability.org/essay/peacebuilding. Accessed on 27 June 2016.

Mamdani, Mahmood. 2017. *Citizen and Subject: Contemporary Africa and the Legacy of Late Colonialism, with a New Preface*. Johannesburg and Kampala: Wits University Press and Makerere Institute of Social Research.

Mamdani, Mahmood. 1996. *Citizens and Subjects: Contemporary Africa and the Legacy of Late Colonialism*. Princeton, NJ: Princeton University Press.

Mazrui, Ali A. and Wiafe-Amoako, Francis. 2016. *African Institutions: Challenges to Political, Social, and Economic Foundations of Africa's Development*. Lanham, MD and London: Rowman and Littlefield.

Mitchell, William and Fazi, Thomas. 2017. *Reclaiming the State: A Progressive Vision of Sovereignty for a Post-Neoliberal World*. London: Pluto Press.

Murphy, Sean D. 2005. 'The Doctrine of Preemptive Self-Defense', *Villanova Law Review*, vol. 50, no. 3, pp. 1–50.

Nhema, Alfred and Zeleza, Pual T. (eds.). 2008. *The Resolution of African Conflicts: The Management of Conflict Resolution & Post-Conflict Reconstruction*. Oxford, Athens and Pretoria: James Currey, Ohio University Press and UNISA Press.

Oda, Hiroshi. 2007. 'Peace-Building from Below: Theoretical and Methodological Considerations toward an Anthropological Study on Peace', *Journal of the Graduate School of Letters*, vol. 2, pp. 1–16.

Osiander, Andreas. 2001. 'Sovereignty, International Relations, and the Westphalian Myth', *International Organization*, vol. 55, no. 2, pp. 251–287.

Paffenholz, Thania. 2015. 'Unpacking the Local Turn in Peace-Building: A Critical Assessment towards an Agenda for Future Research', *Third World Quarterly*, vol. 36, no. 5, pp. 857–874.

Paris, Roland. 2010. 'Saving Liberal Peacebuilding', *Review of International Studies*, vol. 36, pp. 337–365.

Paris, Roland. 2004. *At War's End: Building Peace after Civil Conflict*. Cambridge: Cambridge University Press.

Paris, Roland. 2002. 'International Peace-Building and the *Mission Civilisatrice*', *Review of International Studies*, vol. 28, no. 4, pp. 637–656.

Peilouw, Johanis Steny et al. 2015. 'Legal Doctrine Pre-Emptive Military Strike against the Existence of Principles of Self-Defence and Non-Intervention in International Law', *International Journal of Scientific and Research Publications*, vol. 5, no. 12, pp. 589–593.

Poku, Nana and Whitman, Jim (eds.). 2018. *Africa under Neoliberalism*. London and New York: Routledge.

Renan, Ernest. 1991 [1882a]. 'What Is a Nation?', in Homi K. Bhabha (ed.), *Nation and Narration*. London and New York: Routledge, pp. 8–22.

Renan, Ernest. 1882b. 'What Is a Nation', https://www.globalpolicy.org/component/content/article/172/30340.html. Accessed on 7 October 2019.

Reno, Williams. 2008. 'Bottom-Up Statebuilding?', in Charles T. Call and Wanessa Wyeth (eds.), *Building States to Build Peace*. Boulder, CO, and London: Lynn Rienner Publishers.

Richards, Paul. 2005. *No Peace, No War: Anthropology of Contemporary Armed Conflicts*. Ohio: Ohio University Press.

Richmond, Oliver P. 2011. 'Critical Agency, Resistance and Post-Colonial Civil Society', *Cooperation and Conflict*, vol. 46, no. 4, pp. 419–440.

Shittu, Raji. 2015. 'Africa and the Philosophy of the New Partnership for Africa's Development (NEPAD)', *Journal of African Foreign Affairs*, vol. 2, nos. 1–2, pp. 27–48.

Smith, Neil. 2008. 'Comment: Neo-Liberalism: Dominant but Dead', *Focaal: European Journal of Anthropology*, vol. 51, pp. 155–157.

Steinberg, Gerald M. 2012. 'The Limits of Peace Building Theory', in Roger Mac Ginty (ed.), *The Routledge Handbook of Peacebuilding*. London and New York: Routledge, pp. 36–53.

Swatuk, Larry A. 2018. 'Water, Water Everywhere but Not a Drop to Drink (Except for a Price)', in Nana Poku and Jim Whitman (eds.), *Africa under Neoliberalism*. London and New York: Routledge, pp. 115–135.

Sztompka, Piotr. 1993. *The Sociology of Social Change*. Oxford and Cambridge, MA: Blackwell.

Teschke, Benno. 2002. 'Theorising the Westphalian System of States: International Relations from Absolutism to Capitalism', *European Journal of International Relations*, vol. 8, no. 1, pp. 5–48.

Thiessen, Charles. 2011. 'Emancipatory Peace-Building: Critical Response to (Neo)Liberal Trends', in Thomas Matyok, Jessica Senehi and Sean Byrne (eds.), *Critical Issues in Peace and Conflict Studies: Theory, Practice, and Pedagogy*. Lanham, MD and Plymouth: Lexington Books, pp. 115–140.

Thompson, Michael J. 2005. 'The World According to David Harvey', *Democratiya*, vol. 3, pp. 22–27.

Tom, Patrick. 2017. *Liberal Peace and Post-Conflict Peace-Building in Africa*. London: Palgrave Macmillan.

Tutuianu, Simona. 2013. *Towards Global Justice: Sovereignty in an Interdependent World*. The Hague: Asser Press.

Watson, Adam. 1990. 'Systems of States', *Review of International Studies*, vol. 16, pp. 99–109.

Wiegratz, Jörg, Martiniello, Giuliano and Greco, Elisa. 2018. 'Introduction: Interpreting Changes in Neoliberal Uganda', in Jörg Wiegratz, Giuliano Martiniello and Elisa Greco (eds.), *Uganda: The Dynamics of Neoliberal Transformation*. London: Zed Books, pp. 1–40.

Zambakari, Christopher. 2016. 'Challenges of Liberal Peace and Statebuilding in Divided Societies', *Conflict Trends*, no. 4, pp. 18–24.

Zaum, Dominik. 2012. 'Statebuilding and Governance: The Conundrum of Legitimacy and Local Ownership', in Devon Curtis and Gwinyayi Dzinesa (eds.), *Peace-Building, Power, and Politics in Africa*. Athens: Ohio University Press, pp. 47–62.

2 Neoliberal peacebuilding and statebuilding

Introduction

As explained in the preceding chapter, my focus is on neoliberal peace-building and statebuilding (PBSB). Hence, I will not deal with the various labels related to liberalism and PBSB, such as liberal peace theory, liberal peace, liberal peacebuilding, peacekeeping, peace mediation, conflict prevention and resolution. The chapter constitutes a critiques, following scholars such as Harrison Graham (2010), of the ideological motivated neoliberal social engineering of conflict-stricken societies along the line of Western values and norms.

The theoretical concepts employed to explain and analyse the foundation of neoliberalism in conjunction with interventionist peace-building and statebuilding are invariably ideology, doctrine, social engineering and revolution (Harrison, 2010; Mitchell and Fazi, 2017). This indicates that there is a lack of clear and consensual understanding with regard to what constitutes neoliberal PBSB. In general, however, there is one conception that seems to bring a degree of consensus: Western hegemony. In its economic version, neoliberalism is associated with economic liberalisation, freeing up the market, financial deregulation, anti-inflation measures, macroeconomic stabilisation, privatisation of state-owned enterprises, control of the budget deficit, reduction in fiscal spending, currency devaluation, less state involvement, etc. – issues commonly connected with the Bretton Woods Institutions (Poku and Whitman, 2018; Sandbrook, 2007). This Bretton Woods economic neoliberal prescriptions would subject African economies to naked Western transnational corporations and their African cohort's exploitation. Consequently, the distinct trade mark of neoliberalism became expansionism, interventionism and transgression compelling some to talk about recolonisation.

All this forms the core part of neoliberal PBSB in post-conflict societies. This template of economic reform policy is underpinned by structural adjustment programmes (SAPs). The elevation of neoliberalism to world hegemonic status is associated with the fall of Keynesianism and an assault on the state: the Keynesian model 'started to crumble in the 1970s under the weight of the so-called neoliberal counter-revolution: an ideological war on Keynesianism (which initially took the form of monetarism) waged by a new generation of die-hard free-market economists, mostly based at the University of Chicago, led by Milton Friedman' (Mitchell and Fazi, 2017: 36). It is, however, important to note that neoliberals are not against the state per se, 'but they are instead committed to its total transformation so that it may work perfectly for capital and its accumulation' (Lazzarato, 2015: 70). But Lazzarato maintains that 'capital has never been liberal; it has always been state capital' (Lazzarato, 2015: 69). It is the relationship between capital and state that spurs Western states to pursue interventionist policies and strategies, particularly in resource-endowed fragile societies.

This chapter is about neoliberalism and PBSB. It offers an explanation of how neoliberalism conceptualises PBSB. The literature on the type of PBSB that has come to be known as 'humanitarian interventionism' connects PBSB with liberal and democratic values (Call, 2008; Call and Wyeth, 2008). This literature emerged as dominant in the post-Cold War (and to some degree post-Westphalian) era. Two core values of (neo)liberal democracy are liberal formal elections and a market economy (Paris, 2002). Yet a growing body of evidence indicates that neoliberal PBSB is facing serious challenges (Barnett, 2006; Jarstad and Belloni, 2012; Paris, 1997; Richmond, 2006; Tom, 2017), and particularly in Africa. Interventionist neoliberal PBSB rests on premises of reconstructing war-damaged non-Western societies along the lines of a Western model (Harrison, 2010; Newman et al., 2009; Tom, 2017). Arguably, the spread of neoliberal values and norms in the post-Cold War world came to characterise the main preoccupation of the Western powers – hence the aggressive interventionist statebuilding and peacebuilding policies, strategies and practices targeting developing societies.

Using a number of concepts and perceptions, in this chapter I will analyse how the ideology of neoliberalism is being promoted consciously, intentionally and systematically as the dominant universal ideology applicable to PBSB in conflict-stricken developing societies. I argue that the central tenet of neoliberalism is to reconfigure conflict-ridden and fragile societies in the Western social mould. The chapter consists of six sections. The next section examines the mechanisms, processes and approaches that neoliberalism employs to universalise Western values and norms. There is then an examination of neoliberal peace-building. The next section looks at neoliberal statebuilding; that is followed by a discussion of the neoliberal approach to fixing fragile and failed states. Finally, there is a conclusion.

Socialisation, internalisation and externalisation: the construction of universalism

Neoliberalism is thrust down people's throats as a global human value and norm system that is acceptable (and endorsable) by humans all over the world. Having common human universal values and norms is one thing; but forcing the values and norms of one section of humanity on another is something else altogether. What neoliberalism is trying to do is impose Western values and norms on non-Western societies under the guise of humanitarianism. This section analyses the processes, mechanisms and strategies by which these values and norms are imposed.

The sociological concepts of socialisation, internalisation and externalisation, as an epistemological frame, may help to analyse and explain the universalisation process, by illustrating the process and mechanism by which universalism is constructed. This section therefore draws on the sociological tradition of socialisation, internalisation and externalisation to explain how neoliberalism is engaged in the construction of universal values and norms, particularly in conjunction with PBSB. This sociological tradition (Appelrouth and Edles, 2008; Berger and Luckmann, 1966; Easa and Fincham, 2012) provides some explanation for the formation and construction of values and norms that govern society. Every society develops values and norms that define it and glue its social fabric together. Values and norms are society's bricks and mortar, which is why each society expends a great deal of resources, energy and time on constructing its own values and norms (Durkheim, 1984). The neoliberal interventionist transplantation of Western values and norms amounts to an attempt to unravel the threads binding the target society. This is why neoliberal interventionist PBSB aggravates conflict and post-conflict situations in developing societies.

Looking at the three concepts, *socialisation* refers to the process of learning socially accepted and established knowledge, information, norms, values and practice. *Internalisation* relates to the internal assimilation of what has been learned: this pertains to the 'I', 'me' distinction. *Externalisation*, on the other hand, involves bringing out what has been internalised. It refers to the objectification of the subjective. Once it is externalised or objectified, it assumes universality, whereby no single person or society can claim ownership.

The whole process works in the same way on a global systemic level as it does on a social–psychological (individual, group) level, through operations of learning, internalising and externalising Western values and norms, so that they become global or universal values and norms. It is a mechanism of soft power, by which non-Western societies are reconfigured as pseudo-Western societies: made amenable, malleable, controlled, directed and steered towards a desired societal formation, or social construction of reality (Berger and Luckmann, 1966). To achieve this aim, a variety of mechanisms, instruments and institutions are duly deployed: the media, education, technology, books, films and the film industry, religion and religious institutions, culture and cultural artefacts, material products, symbols, lifestyles, gadgets, soft and hard power. Today, these traditional means are supplemented by information technology, social media and smart phones. This is intended to translocate and root out norms and values deemed to be primitive (or at least not up to the standards of the West) and to induce what anthropologists term mental disposition (Geertz, 1973). To emphasise the role of the film industry in the dissemination of American values and norms, Hollywood is often referred to by the USA as its most important ambassador. This is so because, people throughout the world consume Hollywood products. The consumption of Western cultural product, mediated by modern technology is an effective tool of socialisation and internalisation. The innocent consumers, unaware, are trapped in the cultural production which finally becomes difficult for them to differentiate from their own, which certainly leads to crisis of identity as well as aspiration to flee to the West. The youth mass migration from Africa to the West, seen in recent years, could be understood as an expression of the phenomenon.

The triple sources of universalisation were developed within the fields of sociology and social psychology, particularly by the Chicago School and theorists such as George H. Mead, Herbert Blumer, Erving Goffman, Harold Garfinkel and Robert Merton (Maines, 1977; Serpe and Stryker, 2011; Wiley, 2003). Symbolic interactionism, for instance, expounds the fundamentals of how norms and values are generated, reproduced, maintained and transferred to future generations. The projection from the present to the future occurs through the production of unchallenged and unchallengeable universal ethics. The transition from a social–psychological (individual, group) level to a macro-sociological (societal, continental and global) level occurs in a refined, systematic and coordinated manner. The difference is that, while the micro-level is often inherently domestic, the macro-sociological level (continental and global) is driven by neoliberal intervention and is alien. The alienness is what interests us here – not only as a model of PBSB, but also as a mechanism for reconfiguring conflict-ridden fragile societies in the Western mould. Socialisation, internalisation and externalisation, as mechanisms and processes for creating universal values and norms that coalesce around Western values and norms within a regime of neoliberalism, occur simultaneously at the macro- and the micro-levels. Only once entrenched at both levels can they retain longevity.

In a nutshell, the means and mechanisms of disseminating and fostering those values and norms at the micro- and macro-level, and also the shift from the micro-level to the macro-level (national, continental, global), follow the same pattern. In other words, the socialisation, internalisation and externalisation of Western values and norms by neoliberalism follow the same pattern as occurs at the family, community and national levels, when ideals of personhood, ethics, identity, nationhood and citizenry are inculcated. In this case global citizenry is manufactured, albeit, around Western values and norms that negate the non-Western citizenry. The following section analyses neoliberal peacebuilding, as embedded in the mechanisms and processes highlighted in this section.

Neoliberal peacebuilding

Generally and temporality wise, the genesis of peacebuilding is connected to the post-Cold War era. Indeed, in its normative and multilateral context, it may be attributed to *An Agenda for Peace 1992*, proposed by the UN Secretary-General, Boutros Boutros-Ghali. This provided a kind of blueprint on how the international community would consolidate post-conflict peacebuilding (Tanabe, 2017). Liberal peacebuilding conceptualised as the transplantation of Western models of social, political and economic institutions is taken as a universal method necessary for permanent, liberal-economic and political governance for conflict-shattered states (Heathershaw, 2008). The liberal prefix of peacebuilding was, however, replaced with neo-prefix in the post-Cold War era, a prefix that symbolised an aggressive, hegemonic and interventionist ideology obsessed with moulding conflict-shattered societies along Western mould (Harrison, 2010).

In the area of peacebuilding, neoliberalism has become a doctrine that is translated into what is today commonly known as liberal peace-building, or interventionist humanitarian peacebuilding. For critics, it is an imperialist agenda disguised as humanitarianism. One of the critics, Roland Paris (1997: 56), for instance, noted that the way neo-liberalism operates is, in effect, as 'an enormous experiment in social engineering – an experiment that involves transplanting Western mod-els of social, political, and economic organisation into war-shattered states in order to control civil conflicts: in other words, pacification through political and economic liberalisation'. He further noted else-where that 'peacebuilding agencies transmit such ideas from the core to the periphery of the international system, these agencies are, in ef-fect, involved in an effort to remake parts of the periphery in the im-age of the core' (Paris, 2002: 639). It is therefore considered, 'ethically bankrupt, subject to double standards, coercive and conditional, acul-tural, unconcerned with social welfare, and unfeeling and insensitive towards its subject' (Thiessen, 2011: 118). Understood against our soci-ological concepts of socialisation, internalisation and externalisation (the trinity) and as a purposive and intentional act of reconfiguration of the 'subject', it make great sense.

Several international organisations (IOs) – the UN, international non-governmental organisations (INGOs), NGOs, donors, the World Bank (WB), the International Monetary Fund (IMF) and think tanks – are actively engaged in the transmission and diffusion of the neolib-eral values and norms (Chandler, 2013: 19; Ibhawoh and Akinosho, 2018; Kingsbury, 2019). It is reported that 'the World Bank started to facilitate state- and peacebuilding, financing the disarmament, demo-bilization and reintegration of ex-combatants, as well as mine survey and awareness projects' (Viterbo, 2018: 113). The IOs are part of what is called liberal NGO peacebuilding enterprise (Paffenholz, 2015: 860; Tanabe, 2017), which mediates neoliberal ideology through training, capacity building, providing toolbox blueprints and advising local and international peacebuilding practitioners. This forms part of their job description: the socialisation of those war-torn societies into neoliber-alism. The intended upshot of all this is the creation of a homogenised global world (Carmody and Owusu, 2018). A post-conflict constitution is drafted by Western experts and usually contains concepts such as free and fair elections, civil liberties, judicial independence and due process, rule of law, good governance, etc.; this is later endorsed by national legislation (Paris, 2002: 644). This is grounded on the phil-osophical assumption of standardised, universalistic values (Tanabe, 2017), a universality highly contested. The question is does this address the needs of the rural population, for instance, in Africa? The right response to the question would be it does not, because the rural majority finds itself rendered alien to that neoliberal dispensation that benefit the urban elite. Indigenous local institutions and authorities are consciously and systematically undermined. In Sierra Leone, for instance, 'village and chiefdom development committees are no longer accepted as implementing partners because they are generally considered to be 'corrupt' (Fanthorpe, 2005: 36). This position by donors is taken against the perception of the Sierra Leonean government which was 'chiefdoms are still needed to perform essential local functions, notably the administration of customary land rights, revenue collection, maintenance of law and order' (Fanthorpe, 2005: 35).

A colonial mentality exists in the way post-conflict societies are regarded as objects suitable for a classical civilising mission: African societies are treated as a blank sheet, to be filled by external peacebuilders selecting their ingredients from the Western toolkits. In a symptomatic paternalistic approach, the existence of local rules, institutions, mechanisms, practice, etc. is either denied, or is simply perceived as unfit for purpose. Statebuilding is regarded as democratic if it entails the construction of liberal/neoliberal institutions, and if it pursues formal, regular, liberal multiparty elections that foster peace and peacebuilding (Thiessen, 2011). Accordingly, the restructuring and reconfiguration of the state take place with the aim of promoting neoliberal peacebuilding. Local peacebuilders have to be socialised in these neoliberal norms and values, and need ultimately to internalise them as universal values and norms. Hence the locals were regularly trained to socialise them in the techniques and instruments of neoliberal peacebuilding. Moreover, the external peacebuilders assume responsibility for constructing a state that guarantees peace through the harnessing of neoliberal peacebuilding. According to neoliberalism, liberal statebuilding is a prerequisite for liberal peace (Call and Wyeth, 2008). The problem with all this is that it is devoid of any social, political, historical, cultural and economic indigenous institutions, structures and mechanisms that foster mechanical connection, rather than an organic one. In other words, it is an attempt to transplant alien bodies that, in the long run, produce cleavages between the neoliberal reconstructed state and the larger society.

In short, the successful processing of the trinity – socialisation, internalisation and externalisation –which the training of the locals is to achieve is eventually expected to produce universality. Once the processing is complete, it assumes the status of 'taken for granted', whereby no one will question it and it becomes easy to sell to anyone. Even the people at the receiving end of the imposition begin to believe in it as a solution to their problem. Once this is achieved, no one will be able to oppose neoliberal peacebuilding. This is why international neoliberal peacebuilding rarely inspires serious opposition from the global south, particularly the political elite. Neoliberalism, since the end of the Cold War, has been engaged in a systematic and concerted attempt – through both peaceful and coercive means – to achieve universalisation of Western norms and values, making them an uncontested, universal, epistemic body (Harrison, 2010; Tom, 2017). The effort is not only limited to theoretical or ideological dissemination, but also extends to practical operation through, for instance, structural adjustment programmes (SAPs), and in some cases military invasions that aim to limit the state (Barnett, 2006: 89; Mitchell and Fazi, 2017) or to bring about regime change using and supporting friendly rebel forces (Chetail and Jutersonke, 2015: 7). The doctrine of regime change to bring to power friendly groups conversant with or amenable to neoliberal techniques and ideology became one of the instruments, although tailored in the language of humanitarian peacebuilding or responsibility to protect (R2P). The NATO invasion of Libya, in 2011, that deposed Gaddafi and brought the rebels to power is a case in point of the regime change policy dressed in the R2P garment (Campbell, 2013).

What makes it worrisome is that evidence is concocted to justify the regime change driven intervention. Moreover, the effect of SAPs on political economy is evident in the effective curtailment of the role of the state. One of the mechanisms for curtailing, or rolling back, state involvement in social policies is through the privatisation of key national resources, whereby the wings of the state are clipped and it is not able to engage in development activities or to deliver peace and peacebuilding. The recommendations and impositions of austerity measures by the Bretton Woods institutes on already fragile states further exacerbates the precarious state–society relationship. This is because allegedly the state in Africa cannot be trusted. All this is accompanied by traducement of the post-colonial state as corrupt, prependal, patrimonial, predatory, criminal, ineffective, etc., without interrogating the role of Western powers (e.g. Christensen and Laitin, 2019). Consequently, heavy industry is replaced by a service economy that is run by private actors – foreigners in cahoots with the political elite. Africans produce what they do not consume and consume what they do not produce (Swatuk, 2018: 122). Rarely will this promote enduring peace and peacebuilding.

Western social sciences have been engaged in the production of knowledge geared to ensuring Western global domination and undermining the post-colonial state, thus hampering enduring and meaningful peace and peacebuilding. Highlighting this, Patrick Chabal (2017: 27–28) notes:

> Indeed I reached the conclusion that African cultures have exposed Western social science for what it is: an ill-conceived attempt to apply to the continent the theories that have been developed to explain the West's social and political development. In other words, the study of Africa made plain to me that social sciences as taught and practiced in the West are but a way to force the non-West into the Western experience. Or, to put it another way, social sciences are built on the assumption that modernization means Westernization.

It is this unruly prescription and transplantation of knowledge produced in a specific social setting – spatio-temporal, historical, socio-cultural, political, philosophical and theoretical experience – and translated into an operative mechanism in an entirely different setting that render it extremely problematic. The pervasiveness of the neoliberal ideology in the post-Cold War era has led some to talk of neoliberal revolution (Harrison, 2010). The connotation of revolution in the neoliberal doctrine is intended to express the profound change it seeks to bring about. Harrison further notes:

> This is the essence of social engineering: neoliberal intervention aims to destabilise existing habits (expressed within neoliberal discourse as a hostility to bureaucracy and a desire for good governance, for example) and to produce notions of conduct based on efficiency, transparency and utility.
>
> (Harrison, 2010: 75)

One of the strategies used to enshrine neoliberalism as a universal hegemony is the claim that liberal democracies are inherently more peaceful (Hameiri, 2014) and that peace is a universal human need. Therefore, enshrining neoliberalism as a universal order, reaching every corner of the world, is a noble mission; and it is also the solemn responsibility of those who already enjoy it to spread it. The idea that liberal democracies are inherently peaceful and do not go to war (at least against each other), a Kantian notion is only half true. First, since its breakthrough by the mid-18th century, Western liberal democracies waged war among themselves for hundreds of years (including World

War I and World War II). Noting this, Knapp and Footitt (2013: 2) write,

> Democracies, democratic peace theory suggest, do not go to war against other democracies. Yet since 1914 democracies have repeatedly found themselves embroiled in wars, great or small, whether to defend their colonial possession, their economic and strategic interests, or even their national territory against other power, less democratic and less satisfied with the prevailing international system. Such wars have great potential to subvert democratic values.

Secondly, Western powers are still waging wars outside their borders in Somalia, South Sudan, Mali, Afghanistan, Iraq, Libya and Syria, to mention just a few places. Perhaps it is this waging of wars outside ones borders, that lead to a replacement of the claim 'democracies do not go to war' notion, by 'democracies go to war they win' notion. Dan Reiter and Allan C. Stam, in a book titled *Democracies at War* (2002: 10) state, 'We assume that states pick their fight: they start war when the stakes are high enough, and when they are confident they will win'. They further note, 'Our central argument is that democracies win wars because of the offshoots of public consent and leaders' accountability to voters' (2002: 3). We could easily infer then, neoliberals never hesitate to unleash wars when they are sure they have the means to win and can convince their domestic audience. The role of Western mainstream media, particularly in the United States of America, is really decisive in influencing public opinion when the Pentagon wages war outside the US borders. The role of Western mainstream media of the USA war in Iraq, in 2003, and NATO's war in Libya, in 2011, are clear testimonies of whitewashing of wars waged by liberal democracies. The ability to win a war constitutes the deterrence rather than principles and democratic ideals. This is a real peril to humanity in an era where the dictates of geostrategic calculus determine international relations. But also in an era where powerful states possess highly advanced war technology such as drones that does not require deploying human power on the battle field. This may lead to easy temptation to spark a war, since there will be none or minimal human loss from the powerful side, but also it precludes moral qualm that incurs the killing of a human fellow because the killer would not see the one being killed. It is simply turned into a technical and bureaucratic undertaking, devoid of any human feeling. Explicating the development of the modern means of killing that exonerate personal responsibility, the sociologist Zygmunt Bauman, notes,

> More, however, than the sheer quantity of tools of destruction, even their technical quality, what matters was the way in which they were deployed. Their formidable effectiveness, relied mostly on the subjection of their use to purely bureaucratic, technical considerations (which made their use all but totally immune to the countervailing pressures, such as they might have been submitted to if the means of violence were controlled by dispersed and unco-ordinated agents and deployed in a diffuse way). Violence has been turned into a technique. Like all techniques, it is free from emotions and purely rational. 'It is, in fact, entirely reasonable, if "reason" means instrumental reason, to apply American military force, B-52's, napalm, and all the rest to "communist-dominated" Viet-Nam (clearly an "undesirable object"), as the "operator" to transform it into a "desirable object".
>
> (Bauman, 2000: 98)

Analogically, a drone operator located somewhere in the USA, tasked with eliminating "undesirable" Al Shebab, in Somalia, presses a button and unleashes a deadly monster bomb, that kills innocent civilian bystanders, is shielded by bureaucratic and technical rationality. If, instead, the operator is not shielded by bureaucratic and technical rationality, and more importantly, if he or she was to face physically his innocent victims would that person behave the same way? Certainly, modern technology of waging wars denies us one of the salient elements that make us human, emotion.

Our common humanity becomes then contingent on who wins and dominates. The preaching of a common humanity should include a prohibition on waging war against all, not just against liberal democracies or wars that could only be won because of resources.

The peacebuilding project as prescribed by neoliberalism is expected to promote the market economy and electoral multiparty democracy. The 1990s were a watershed in the triumphant neoliberal discourse: liberal discourse was replaced by aggressive neoliberal discourse and narratives. This aggressive discourse picked up momentum and currency following the 9/11 attacks on the United States (Barnett, 2006: 87; Harrison, 2010). Some also call the aggressive interventionist venture the 'post-modern imperialist scheme' (Henderson, 2015: 256–257). Richmond (2013: 308) notes: 'Processes of peacebuilding and statebuilding are designed to develop a liberal social contract in contrast to the predatory state that mainstream state formation expects.' Neoliberalism's crusade against the so-called 'predatory' state denies developing societies the rights and options of designing, experimenting with and operating their own paths for constructing and reconstructing their own developmental trajectory, including PBSB. This lack of contextualisation quite often highlights neoliberal interventions. Richard Jackson (2018: 2), for instance notes:

> First it [peacebuilding] has been criticised for operating according to a standardised blueprint which does not take into account the unique historical and cultural settings in which it is applied. As Mac Ginty puts it, 'the liberal peace is operationalized in highly standardized formats that leave little space for alternative approaches', follows 'set templates' in applying reforms, and adopts 'a formulaic path' which often fails to take account of local actors and their preferences and contextual knowledge.

It is this attitude that compels many to dub neoliberal peacebuilding a 'new imperialism' (Jackson, 2018; Shittu, 2015) or a 'civilising mission' (Paris, 2002).

In Africa, the construction of war-shattered societies along the Western mould, failed to bring lasting peace. In Angola, for instance, neoliberal inspired peacebuilding initiative sparked war, 'the UN oversaw postwar election in 1992 that [instead] provoked one of the former belligerents to resume fighting, in part because there were no institutional mechanisms established to resolve disputes over election (Paris, 2010: 341). One should, perhaps add, indigenous institutions and mechanisms of conflict resolution were ignored. Subsequently, Angola was plunged into a bloody civil war with colossal consequences to the society (Ngongo, 2012). With regard to South Sudan, Wambugu (2019: 12), notes 'an international engagement that interacted and continued to interact with South Sudan from the premise of an incapable partner, while overlooking the role of the community receiving intervention, perhaps of the greatest tragedies of international liberal peacebuilding approaches'. Earlier, in the case of Mozambique, neoliberal peacebuilding did not achieve the needed outcome (Sabaratnam, 2011). Indeed, 'More than two decades of peacebuilding processes in Mozambique have shown that there is no clear-cut way to ensure the sustainability of peace in the country' (Reppell et al., 2016: 25).

The demise of the Soviet Union and the end of the Cold War spurred a frenzy of triumphalism among right-wing scholars. Francis Fukuyama (1992) declared the 'end of history' and announced the universality of liberal democracy. Samuel Huntington also published a book in 1996 about the clash of civilisations, in which he proposed the reordering of the world. According to Huntington, the demise of socialism brought a reconfiguration of the world, pitching humans along civilisations. According to his perception, the demise of socialism brought to an end the struggle of two ideologies that had, up to then, propelled human history. This then, according to Huntington, ushered in a new era when civilisations are pitted against each other. To entrench the neoliberal era, not only was it imperative to defeat remaining socialist states (China and Cuba), but also was imperative to remould the African state with the track record of association with the socialist states.

It was in this supposed new era that post-Cold War peacebuilding was geared to neoliberal democracy and market economy norms and values. To buttress the neoliberal peacebuilding, the state was side-lined and a range of non-state actors – IOs, NGOs, CS, opposition, etc. (Barnett, 2006; Newman et al., 2009: 7) – were mandated to play active roles in neoliberal peacebuilding. This is so because the state is not to be trusted (Tom, 2017: 66). Many works appeared that supported concerted assaults on the state and concepts such as predator state, criminal state, patrimonial state, shadow state, etc. were popularised and promoted (Bayarat, 1993; Bratton and de Walle, 1997; Chabal and Daloz, 1999; Christensen and Laitin, 2019; Englebert, 2000; Herbst, 2000; Hyden, 2013). The anti-state attitude that increasingly assumed prominence sought to promote the idea of rolling back the state, and of locating strategic functions and roles in the spheres of non-state actors.

Some of the characteristic features of neoliberal peacebuilding are described as formalist, technical and administrative in nature (Chandler, 2013). As formalist, it is grounded on pre-determined and imported premises. It usually, therefore, operates on the basis of checklists. One such lists includes reforming the security forces, police, intelligence, army, etc., and the process of demobilisation, disarmament and reintegration (DDR) also assumes prominence (Barnett, 2006; Conteh-Morgan, 2004; Curtis and Dzinesa, 2012; Grävingholt et al., 2009; Jackson, 2018; Omach, 2012). Nevertheless, rarely do these measures seek to tackle the root causes of these conflicts and consequently contribute veritably to lasting peace and peacebuilding. International financial institutions (IFIs) have borne the lion's share of the funding: 'the World Bank started to facilitate State- and peacebuilding, financing the disarmament, demobilisation and reintegration of ex-combatants, as well as mine survey and awareness projects' (Viterbo, 2018: 113). It is clear, then, that this reformist approach focuses on technical and temporary solutions. It mainly concerns immediate post-conflict solution and the reconciliation of combatants (Jackson, 2018). In doing this, it (wittingly or unwittingly) ignores the root causes of conflicts. Moreover, the concentration on technical solutions neglects the profoundly political nature of conflicts and of the concomitant peacebuilding. Emphasising this, Thania Paffenholz (2015: 861) notes 'International liberal peacebuilding becomes an inherently conservative undertaking, which seeks managerial solutions to fundamental conflicts over resources and power.' Other dimensions ignored include inequality, development, ethnic relations, global power structures and relations, which are requisite for positive peace. By admitting the political nature of conflict, PBSB would require political and enduring measures of resolution to be sought, rather than technical and temporary measures; it would also mean addressing the root causes of conflicts. Peacebuilding that follows a peace agreement is constrained by the need to consolidate and institutionalise the deal, even if it is deficient in certain respects. In addition, the process is characterised by an overdependence on external experts, which devalues indigenous knowledge, experts and authorities (Thiessen, 2011). It is often the case that external actors assume the role of defining the issues and deciding who should be included and involved in the peace process. But this approach denies the subjects ownership and agency (Curtis, 2012), and therefore precludes lasting solutions.

The donor conference has increasingly assumed prominence as a mechanism for bringing together the necessary resources to achieve peacebuilding. It is as if money is the panacea (although no doubt it helps). Anyway, donors' pledges of funds are never completely fulfilled, which is why the implementation of many peace agreements suffers from a shortage of cash. There is no sound evidence that donor conferences and external resources guarantee peace, peacebuilding and statebuilding. On the contrary, there is ample evidence that donor-driven solutions often end in failure. Somalia may be a good example: in spite of several dozen international conferences, the country is no closer to peace. Moreover, most of the fund is misappropriated leading to distortions of the socio-economic structure and the statebuilding process. An illustration of this could be provided by this long quote below,

> Things were looking up for Afghanistan. A majority of the Afghan people were longing to leave the Taliban behind. The international community thought that all that Afghanistan needed now was a large infusion of foreign aid. Representatives from the United Nations and several leading NGOs soon descended on the capital, Kabul.

What ensued should not have been a surprise, especially given the failure of foreign aid to poor countries and failed states over the past five decades. Surprise or not, the usual ritual was repeated. Scores of aid workers and their entourages arrived in town with their own private jets, NGOs of all sorts poured in to pursue their own agendas, and high-level talks began between governments and delegations from the international community. Billions of dollars were now coming to Afghanistan. But little of it was used for building infrastructure, schools, or other public service essential for the development of inclusive institutions or even for restoring law and order. While much of the infrastructure remained in tatters, the first tranche of the money was used to commission an airline to shuttle around UN and other international officials. The next thing they needed were drivers and interpreters. So they hired the few English-speaking bureaucrats and the remaining teachers in Afghan schools to chauffeur and chaperone them around, paying them multiples of current Afghan salaries. As the few skilled bureaucrats were shunted into jobs servicing the foreign aid community, the aid flows, rather than building infrastructure in Afghanistan, started by undermining the Afghan state they were supposed to build upon and strengthen.

(Acemoglu and Robinson, 2013: 451)

This could be taken as confirmation of the failure of neoliberal intervention's concern with conflict and the post-conflict situation, where the focus is on preventing the resumption or escalation of violent conflict, without taking seriously the profound root causes. This focus neglects the long-term and sustainable process. This short-term focus of neoliberal PBSB is an indication of the unsustainability of neoliberal-driven peace (Tom, 2017). As another commentator says,

the reality of neo-liberalism in Africa is so closely associated with external intervention, from early imperial ventures in the nineteenth century to recently Northern-imposed development programs, that much of the essay's discussion of governmentality, citizenship, and 'governmental interventions' seems out of context in a region where most governments are struggling to maintain territorial sovereignty and national budgets are frighteningly dependent on foreign/external aid. African citizens and leaders, in turn, have learned to mimic the rhetoric of externally imposed neo-liberalism to access resources.

(Little, 2008: 149)

The mimicking may impede Africans from searching for innovative domestic solutions. The negative attitude to neoliberal PBSB, then, is not only because it is predicated on arbitrary imposition, but also because it has led African citizens and leaders – and primarily African scholars – to mimic its rhetoric. This is an indication of how the neoliberal model has in recent years grown so dominant that even those subjected to its imprudence uncritically rehearse it. In other words, it proves the success of the socialisation, internalisation and externalisation of neoliberal values and norms.

To add to the confusion,

> it has been suggested that, in many aspects, the liberal peacebuilding model is probably more accurately conceived of as a *statebuilding* project, rather than a *peace*building project in the peace theory sense. Analysts point to the 'fetishization of state and institution-building', the way that 'internationally led peace-support interventions fail to transcend a top-down bias', and the fact that 'statebuilding is far more focused on security and market institutions than on representative, democratic norms or human rights.
> (Jackson, 2018: 2–3, emphasis in original)

Jackson (2018: 3) goes on:

> liberal peace(state)building can be seen as a continuation of longer historical processes of imperialism, neo-colonialism and Western-isation, in that 'liberal peace has followed liberal imperialism in asserting a superior moral order, knowledge, justice and freedom and devaluing, indeed discounting, local experience of peace and politics'. At the same time, 'Local participation, ownership identity, norms, and historical systems of power, social organisation and peacemaking are excluded by this version of peacebuilding. Peace instead reflects Western/Northern concerns and priorities.'

Neoliberal peacebuilding, as the quotes above demonstrate, is also conceptualised in association with statebuilding. Statebuilding itself is understood in a technical sense, as a requirement for peace and peacebuilding. PBSB, as we will see later, however, could display discord, compelling us to seriously take note of the difference. Beyond the discord between PBSB, the most serious deficiency of neoliberal peacebuilding is its reliance on foreign models, historical experiences, knowledge, expertise and institutional foundations, which quite often fail to address the imperatives of peace and peacebuilding in Africa.

Indeed, it is contributing to the growing perception that neoliberalism is a Western tool of neo-imperialism, recolonisation and the scramble for African resources. The next section analyses neoliberal statebuilding.

Neoliberal statebuilding

The relationship between PBSB is a highly contested area. The harmony and discord is discussed in Chapter 5. This section focuses on the neoliberal conception of statebuilding in fragile and conflict-ridden societies. In the neoliberal model of SB, ideology is more dominant as an overarching approach than science or theory. Both classical and contemporary theories of statebuilding are markedly absent, not to mention theories and models relevant to developing society realities. Accordingly, the foundation of neoliberal interventionist statebuilding rests on experiences brought from other historical, cultural, socioeconomic, political and philosophical societal settings. This makes it permeated with normativity and ideology, but less of science and rigorous empirical data, normativity and ideology the target people could not recognise and identify with.

As with neoliberal peacebuilding, so neoliberal statebuilding came to prominence in the post-Cold War, post-Westphalian era, particularly in the late 1980s. The development that underpinned the proliferation of neoliberal interventionist statebuilding could be traced to two factors. First, the Soviet Union collapsed, which heralded the triumph of liberal democracy and the defeat of state socialism. This paved the way for Western powers to interfere in the internal affairs of states in the developing world. It is this interference in the internal affairs of sovereign states that is seen by some scholars as commencement in the post-Westphalian Treaty (Thiessen, 2011; Tutuianu, 2013). The Westphalian Treaty, which constrained and regulated inter-state relations, was violated at whim (Bendana, 2006). Second, many states in the developing world entered a period of fragility, weakness, crisis and collapse, leading to failure to meet their basic responsibilities and functions. These states not only failed to provide society with peace, security and development, but even posed a danger to society. Moreover, beyond their national borders, these failed states posed a danger to the wider world. This at least was the perception of the Western powers and warranted intervention. The two factors together formed the perfect excuse for the Western powers to intervene and to reconstruct and reconfigure the failed states in their own image, to the extent of engineering their collapse (Bendana, 2006) – as in the case of Libya (Campbell, 2013). Many are convinced that 'Statebuilding seems to become a matter of introducing Western norms of liberal, market-oriented governance' (Bendana, 2006: 41). The reconstruction and reconfiguration of these states in the Western mould could not be achieved subscribing to certain models, mechanisms, approaches, strategies and methodologies. Certainly, as critics of neoliberal interventionist statebuilding point out, the imposition of foreign elements further aggravated state crisis, fragility and failure.

Quite often – at least in the short term – these foreign elements fail to work. As was indicated earlier, the neoliberal interventionist imposition of statebuilding is characterised by short-term technical, administrative, foreign-expert-based management, quick fixes and elitist and top-down approaches (Jackson, 2018; Thiessen, 2011). The absolute dominance of the neoliberal state, which 'collapses the notion of freedom into freedom for economic elites' (Thompson, 2005: 23), provides the foundation for the triumph of global neoliberalism. In the technical, neoliberal understanding, statebuilding is reduced to good governance, which offers technical solutions to very political problems (Bendana, 2006). Good governance is important, but it is not the whole remedy; it is reductionist. Governance is about administering, not about government or state. Good administration, no doubt, is important, but could not replace statebuilding. Statebuilding concerns institution building as well as distribution of power. These attributes are the essence of state crisis that drive conflicts.

Neoliberalism prescribes state decentralisation, where the concentration of power at the centre is perceived to be an obstacle, and instead power is devolved to regions. Deriving from its general ideological position of the post-nation state, neoliberalism's vision of an alternative model of statebuilding (if it has one) is of a decentralised, weak state that offers ample space for non-state actors, such as the IMF, WB, CS, NGOs and other social groups, such as youth and women. Functional democratic institutions (neoliberal), rule of law, market economy and property rights form the foundations of the statebuilding reforms. These reforms are geared to the benefit of transnational corporates through privatisation, foreign direct investment, deregulation and liberalisation of the monetary system. The creation of a conducive environment for international capital undermines the state, since it prevents the state from being able to deliver basic societal provisions. In many African countries, INGOs have overtaken delivery of basic services, undermining state legitimacy. This political economy of statebuilding, itself, is a source of fragility. Ultimately, the neoliberal state is delegitimised in popular eyes. As Bendana (2006: 42) notes, 'In truth, under neoliberalism, statebuilding becomes state-dismantling as power is turned over to transnational corporations and to the un-elected bureaucrats of the global institutions such as IMF, World Bank and WTO – a process of national and State disempowerment.' Neoliberal interventionist statebuilding is against the very notion of a strong state.

Post-conflict and conflict neoliberal interventionist statebuilding suffers from a lack of popular legitimacy. Confirming this assertion, Lakhdar Brahimi (2007: 7) notes: 'In Iraq, the institutions created by invaders and the Iraqis drafted to serve under occupation never acquired any legitimacy or credibility in the eyes of the people of Iraq.' Local forces installed by external intervention and made responsible for post-conflict statebuilding generally lack any mandate from society. It could be said the same about Somalia where the federal constitution, institutions and government imposed by external actors never garnered popular legitimacy. This is because they are selected by external actors, and so they alienate many communities and stakeholders who are not on friendly terms with the external actors. Furthermore, external actors also dictate the non-participation of those they perceive as antagonists. Thus the Taliban (Afghanistan), Sunni (Iraq) and Al-Shabaab (Somalia) were excluded from the relevant peace processes on the instructions of external actors. This exclusionary measure unquestionably ensures perpetuation of the conflict. Seventeen years after the demise of Saddam Hussein, Iraq is still paying the price of the invasion. The real question is then what really did the envisioning achieve? In addition, the presence of external military forces in support of one side of the conflict – Americans (Iraq), Americans and NATO (Afghanistan), Ethiopia and Kenyan forces (Somalia), NATO (in support of rebels in Libya) – hampers negotiations and the reconciliation of antagonists, thereby denying the statebuilding process domestic ownership and representativity. The case of DRC is a good example of the presence of external military forces (Eriksen, 2009). The neighbouring countries' military involvement in support of one or another group has prolonged the conflict in DRC.

The coexistence of external actors (whose primary goal it is to install a friendly elite group at the helm of state power) and a predatory elite (whose main ambition is to pounce on the benefits to be accrued by occupying state power) renders neoliberal statebuilding precarious. The coexistence relies on their shared interest in excluding non-friendly groups and rival elites – something that only cements the precariousness. The political calculation of expediency thus renders the neoliberal-oriented statebuilding process precarious, conflict-prone, exclusionary, unrepresentative, unstable and unsustainable. The (generally overwhelming) rural population is shut out of the statebuilding process, and so it becomes elitist.

'Neoliberalism has undermined democratisation through the imposition from above of a procedural rather than substantial form of democracy. Moreover, by redefining the structures of governance, neoliberalisation fragments society and alienates people's participation, running against genuine participatory democracy' (Wiegratz et al., 2018: 22). Instead of constructing a viable democratic state, neoliberalism ends up establishing an addendum to the neoliberal world state system, completely uprooted from its societal setting, which further contributes to cleavages, inequalities, tensions and conflicts in society. Some call this type of state Westphalian state (Araoye, 2014). Hence, instead of generating peace, stability, harmony, unity and development, interventionist neoliberal statebuilding fosters further state fragility, conflict, global tensions and instability. The next section analyses neoliberalism's ambition and attempt to fix fragile and failed states.

Fixing fragile and failed states

One of the declared objectives of neoliberal interventionism is fixing fragile and failed states. The challenge, however, is what is fragility and failure, what are the measurements and benchmarks. Moreover, what are the root causes of fragility? These are question that require theoretical, conceptual and empirical clarity, in order to understand the phenomenon, let alone offer solution to it. The concept of fragility is notoriously malleable, imbued with controversy and ambiguity. The source of the controversies and ambiguities is chiefly the lack of a clear definition and conceptualisation. The term 'fragility' is very broadly used: for instance, it is seen as a measure of the extent to which the actual practices and capacities of states differ from their idealised image. Fragility in this sense is a measure of how well (or poorly) the actual institutions, functions and political processes of a state shape up against the strong image of a sovereign state – the one reified in both state theory and international law (Carment and Samy, 2014: 5). Accordingly, 'there are states with capacities to perform some tasks and there are states with no capacities to perform them' (Pureza, 2006: 3). It is a matter of degree, not kind. This notion of fragility is embedded in the widely acknowledged categories of failed states, failing states, collapsed states, fragile states, weak states; 'the concept of the fragile, failed and collapsed states (FFCS) is a product of the neoliberal doctrine' (Pureza, 2006: 1). These statuses are, in turn, gauged against 'effective responsive governance, authority over people and territory, and capacity of the economy and of resource mobilization' (Trauschweizer, 2014: xi). The 'concept of FFCS is an expression of power' (Pureza, 2006: 2). Moreover, the failed state is an *a contrario* concept, defined by analogy with a 'successful state' (Pureza, 2006).

Failed or unstable societies are perceived to be a threat to international security (Barnett, 2006: 87; Newman et al., 2009: 3; Tom, 2017). Dealing with this security threat presupposes mending those failed societies. Failed societies are generally perceived as unable to construct a viable state (or unqualified to have a state at all). In the case of the latter, neoliberalism will construct a state for them; in the case of the former, where the state does not conform to neoliberal values, it will change it for them. Regime change is then followed by the imposition of statebuilding (Caplan, 2007; Downes, 2011), in which the reconstructed state should resemble the neoliberal state. This conceptualisation provides Western powers with legitimate rights to intervene. Hence, 'the label of "failed state" becomes synonymous with an invitation for external intervention and, ironically the reinforcement of the State to serve global forces' (Bendana, 2006: 40). The interventionist measures come with, and go on to foster, their own conceptions and models of peacebuilding.

Oliver Richmond highlights this:

> Orientalism justifies the interventionary and disciplinary character of the liberal peace and statebuilding. It also naturalises the pre-eminence of international legitimacy over local legitimacy. This is despite the fact that state formation debates do not solely imply the state is an instrument of power, but also that it has social, anthropological, and redistributive functions: i.e. it is an instrument of identity and social justice. The state is part of the social world and cannot instrumentally be separated from the broader context provided by local history, culture, and society.
> (Richmond, 2013: 304)

The critical question is are we able to properly and adequately identify the root causes of the fragility of the state? For that matter, are we really interested in identifying the real root causes of fragility? If we identify the real root cause of fragility, are we able (even willing) to really cure them? No attention is paid to indigenous conceptions, institutions, mechanisms and practices of peacebuilding and conflict resolution. Even if attempts are made to pay attention, always fall short of any adequacy. It is worth emphasising the imperatives of paying enough attention to indigenous instruments of peacebuilding in order to achieve sustainable peace. Further, Richmond argues:

> Much of the recent generation of peacebuilding and statebuilding literature has been normative or positivist, focused on problem solving (how to build/fix a peace or state), and understood through the lenses of realism and liberalism. The state is constructed by international actors to respond to state formation tensions, but it is also dependent upon them. Statebuilding provides the state with its security, technical, and bureaucratic infrastructure, whereas peacebuilding shapes its institutions and laws, according to a normative vision of a 'good state'.
>
> (Richmond, 2013: 307)

The neoliberal project of fixing failed states is permeated with shopping lists that are imported from Western metropolitan ideological malls. One feature of the list is that it is usually facilitated by external actors. The preoccupation of external mediators is chiefly with short-term security and stability. A serious problem with the imposition of an external solution is that it is selective in choosing the agenda, the issues and the domestic actors to be involved (Newman et al., 2009: 4). This certainly renders it non-comprehensive, non-inclusive and too short lived to be able to fix failed states. It avoids addressing the root causes; instead, it treats the proximate causes – and may end up dealing with symptoms (Young, 2012). It focuses only on the combatants (Young, 2012), and therefore a whole range of actors and interests are excluded; this undermines the sustainability of the peace deal and post-war reconstruction, and thereby produces regimes devoid of broad legitimacy (Barnett, 2006: 103–104; Menkhaus, 2012). Elements that could ensure a lasting solution – such as social reconciliation, broad participation, inclusiveness, transformation and democratisation – are paid scant attention. These measures require time and resources. The welfare of citizens and development are markedly absent from the solutions (Conteh-Morgan, 2004; Newman et al., 2009). Above all, it is alleged that this approach is driven by and promotes self-interest, alien ideologies and perspectives, at the expense of indigenous mechanisms, institutions, perspectives and authorities that would guarantee that failed states could be fixed permanently. This is so because the indigenous or local actors, practices and cultures are perceived to be 'inferior and an obstacle to the project of liberal and rational governance (Tanabe, 2017: 450). The post-Cold War neoliberalism is also criticised for splitting with classical liberalism. Noting this, Issa Shivji writes,

> Margaret Thatcher [claimed] '... there is no such thing as society. There are individual men and women, and there are families'. The individualism of neo-liberalism is narcissist. It is not even the enlightened individualism of liberalism which stood for individual freedom and the flowering of the individual. Neo-liberalism knows only one freedom – freedom to choose from commodities on offer (Issa Shivji).[1]

According to the proponents of this perspective, classical liberalism – which rests on the core values of liberty, equality and fraternity – was founded on the political philosophy of humanism. The cornerstone of this humanism is the foundation of equality, respect, dignity, recognition and respect of specificity, diversity, values and norms of every society. Neoliberalism is therefore seen as a negation of humanism. It is underscored, 'that neoliberalism has very little to do with classical liberalism or laissez-faire, and certainly did not entail a retreat of the state in favour of the market' (Mitchell and Fazi, 2017: 74). One thing is, however, very clear – its problem-solving orientation:

> orthodox ... approaches to peace-making and peacebuilding emphasize statebuilding and state-reform as their main methodology. This is essentially a 'problem-solving' approach which accepts the parameters or structures within which the conflict occurs and is content to 'fix' the immediate problems without challenging the meta-structures that support the conflict.
>
> (Mac Ginty, 2008: 146)

Finally, it is uncertain if neoliberal peacebuilding intends to address issues such as power, legitimacy, representation and participation – issues that are vital for enduring peace and functional peacebuilding (Newman et al., 2009). Neoliberalism's drive for globalism that engenders totalitarian universalism without the corollary benefits for non-Western societies only produces a segmented, hierarchised, unequal global citizenry. This will not lead to peace, stability and security in Africa or in the wider world, and there is no way that it will be able to provide a remedy for state failure.

Conclusion

This chapter has sought to critically examine neoliberal interventionist PBSB. The triumphant ascension to global domination by neoliberalism is associated with the collapse of state socialism and the end
of the Cold War. Both inside and outside academia, the post-Cold
War concept was popularised. Less influential, yet a trend of the post-
Cold War era, has been the rise of the post-Westphalian concept. The
two concepts undergird the debate, discourse and narratives of the
emergent new world order. The post-Cold War and post-Westphalian
era was to herald the emergence of a single world system embedded
in neoliberalism and characterised by a global common humanity.
Globalism – another fashionable concept that became a catch-all
phrase of the new era – was supposed to be a mechanism that ground
down differences to produce a human species that inhabited a single
identity imbued with the Western norms and values (now relabelled
'universal') that constitute the foundation of neoliberalism; other systems are now proven to be inferior and obsolete.

It is under this self-appointed hegemonic ideology that the interventionist neoliberal PBSB was launched to remedy the pathologies
afflicting conflict-prone societies. The two perceptions guiding neoliberal interventionist PBSB are that failed states are dangerous to their
own societies and are fertile ground for terrorism that affects Western,
and particularly US, security and interests.

Following the end of the Cold War, many societies experienced serious unrest and conflict, with devastating effects that led to state fragility, crisis, failure and collapse. The carnage that was unleashed gave
rise to discourses of humanitarian intervention, responsibility to protect, statebuilding to build peace, and PBSB legitimising interference
in the internal affairs of sovereign states. The violation of sovereignty
was justified by the state's inability to protect its own people –
or worse, its propensity to kill them. This, in turn, paved the way
for the doctrine of regime change. Neoliberal intervention in the internal affairs of sovereign states was facilitated by the demise of the
Westphalian Treaty, which for centuries had guided and regulated the
inter-state system. The Westphalian inter-state system was founded on
the cardinal principle that states – whether big or small – are equal and
legally protected against hostility, interference, invasion, etc. by other
states, particularly powerful ones.

This neoliberal intervention is perceived by the object people as a
disguised new form of colonisation – new imperialism, reminiscent
of the civilising mission. This perception is further enhanced by the

failure on the part of PBSB to achieve its declared objectives. The rise of the global war on terror also proved a one-sided approach to the problem, demonstrating that it is driven by Western interests and definitions, particularly those of the United States of America. The US administration saw any problem arising in any corner of the world as a threat to its interests and security; this entitled it to take pre-emptive measures. Instead of curing the problem, the war on terror aggravated it – or even at times created it. The US global war on terror became one of the destabilising factors in the world.

Neoliberal-driven PBSB is perceived as social engineering, to reconfigure developing societies along Western neoliberal lines, rather than as genuine PBSB, designed to help conflict-prone developing societies. This social engineering aided by the emergence of a world system dictated by post-Cold War and post-Westphalian developments is in no way contributing to PBSB world over, however.

Note

1 'It's the Revolution that matters: Remembering Che': https://www.pambazuka. org/pan-africanism/it%E2%80%99s-revolution-matters-remembering-che.

References

Acemoglu, Daron and Robinson, James A. 2013. *Why Nations Fail: The Origin of Power, Prosperity and Poverty*. London: Profile Books LTD.

Appelrouth, Scott and Edles, Laura Desfor. 2008. *Classical and Contemporary Sociological Theory*. Los Angeles, CA, London, New Delhi and Singapore: Pine Forge Press.

Araoye, Ademola. 2014. *Sources of Conflict in the Post Colonial African State*. Trenton, NJ, London, Cape Town, Nairobi, Addis Ababa, Asmara, Ibadan and New Delhi: African World Press.

Barnett, Michael. 2006. 'Building a Republican Peace: Stabilizing States after War', *International Security*, vol. 30, no. 4, pp. 87–112.

Bauman, Zygmunt. 2000. *Modernity and the Holocaust*. Ithaca, NY: Cornel University Press.

Bayarat, Jean-Francois. 1993. *The State in Africa: The Politics of the Belly*. New York: Longman.

Bendana, Alejandro. 2006. 'Peace-Building and Neoliberalism: Will Foreign Dictated Statebuilding Prevail?', *Journal für Entwicklungspolitik*, vol. 22, no. 3, pp. 35–54.

Berger, Peter L. and Luckmann, Thomas. 1966. *The Social Construction of Reality*. London: Penguin Books.

Brahimi, Lakhdar. 2007. 'State Building in Crisis and Post-Conflict Countries', presented at 7th Global Forum on Reinventing Government, Building Trust in Government, 26–29 June, Vienna, Austria.

Bratton, Michael and De Walle, Nicolas. 1997. *Democratic Experiment in Africa: Regime Transition in Comparative Perspective.* Cambridge: Cambridge University Press.

Call, Charles T. 2008. 'Building States to Build Peace? A Critical Analysis', *Journal of Peace Building and Development*, vol. 4, no. 2, pp. 60–74.

Call, Charles T. and Wyeth, Vanessa (eds.). 2008. *Building States to Build Peace.* Boulder, CO, and London: Lynne Rienner Publishers.

Campbell, Horace. 2013. *Global NATO and the Catastrophic Failure in Libya: Lessons for Africa in the Forging of African Unity.* New York: Monthly Review Press.

Caplan, Richard. 2007. 'From Collapsing States to Neo-Trusteeship: The Limits to Solving the Problem of "Precarious Statehood" in the 21st Century', *Third World Quarterly*, vol. 20, no. 2, pp. 231–244.

Carment, David and Samy, Yiagadeesen. 2014. 'The Future of War: Understanding Fragile States and What to Do about Them', in Ingo Trauschweizer and Steven M. Miner (eds.), *Failed States and Fragile Societies: A New World Order?* Athens: Ohio University Press, pp. 3–27.

Carmody, Padraig and Owusu, Francis. 2018. 'Neoliberalism, Urbanization and Change in Africa', in Nana Poku and Jim Whitman (eds.), *Africa under Neoliberalism.* London and New York: Routledge, pp. 61–75.

Chabal, Patrick. 2017. 'Culture and the Study of Politics in Postcolonial Africa', in Tejumola Olaniyan (ed.), *State and Culture in Postcolonial Africa: Enchantings.* Bloomington, IN: Indiana University Press, pp. 27–54.

Chabal, Patrick and Daloz, Jean-Pascal. 1999. *Africa Works: Disorder as Political Instrument.* Oxford, Bloomington and Indianapolis, IN: James Currey and Indiana University Press.

Chandler, David. 2013. 'Peacebuilding and the Politics of Non-Linearity: Rethinking "Hidden" Agency and "Resistance"', *Peacebuilding*, vol. 1, no. 1, pp. 17–32.

Chetail, Vincent and Jutersonke, Oliver. 2015. 'Peace-Building: A Review of the Academic Literature', White Paper Series no. 19, Geneva Peacebuilding Platform.

Christensen, Darin and Laitin, David D. 2019. *African States since Independence: Order, Development, and Democracy.* New Haven, CT and London: Yale University Press.

Conteh-Morgan, Earl. 2004. 'Peace-Building and Human Security: A Constructivist Perspective', in Hideaki Shinoda and Ho-Won Jeong (eds.), *Conflict and Human Security: A Research for New Approaches of Peacebuilding*, IPSHU English Research Report Series No. 19. Hiroshima: Hiroshima University, pp. 229–251.

Curtis, Devon. 2012. 'The Contested Politics of Peace-Building in Africa', in Devon Curtis and Gwinyayi Dzinesa (eds.), *Peace-Building, Power, and Politics in Africa.* Athens: Ohio University Press, pp. 1–28.

Curtis, Devon and Dzinesa, Gwinyayi (eds.). 2012. *Peace-Building, Power, and Politics in Africa.* Athens: Ohio University Press.

Downes, Alexander B. 2011. 'Regime Change Doesn't Work', *Boston Review*, 1 September.

Durkheim, Emile. 1984. *The Division of Labour in Society*. London: Macmillan Press.

Easa, Nasser Fathi and Fincham, Robin. 2012. 'The Application of the Socialisation, Externalisation, Combination and Internalisation Model in Cross-Cultural Contexts: Theoretical Analysis', *Knowledge and Process Management*, vol. 19, no. 2, pp. 103–109.

Englebert, Pierre. 2000. *State Legitimacy and Development in Africa*. Boulder, CO: Lynne Rienner Publishers.

Eriksen, Stein Sundstol. 2009. 'The Liberal Peace Is Neither: Peace-Building, State Building and the Reproduction of Conflict in the Democratic Republic of Congo', *International Peacekeeping*, vol. 16, no. 5, p. 666.

Fanthorpe, Richard. 2005. 'On the Limits Liberal Peace: Chiefs and Democratic Decentralization in Post-War Sierra Leone', *African Affairs*, vol. 105, no. 418, pp. 27–49.

Fukuyama, Francis. 1992. *The End of History and the Last Man*. New York: Avon Books.

Geertz, Clifford. 1973. *The Interpretation of Cultures*. New York: Fontana Press.

Grävingholt, Järn, Gänzle, Stefan and Ziaja, Sebastian. 2009. 'Policy Brief: Concepts of Peace-Building and State Building – How Compatible Are They?' German Development Institute, 11 March.

Hameiri, Shahar. 2014. 'The Crisis of Liberal Peacebuilding and the Future of Statebuilding', *International Politics*, vol. 51, no. 3, pp. 316–333.

Harrison, Graham. 2010. *Neoliberal Africa: The Impact of Global Social Engineering*. London and New York: Zed Books.

Heathershaw, John. 2008. 'Unpacking the Liberal Peace: The Dividing and Merging of Peacebuilding Discourses', *Millennium: Journal of International Studies*, vol. 36, no. 3, pp. 597–622.

Henderson, Errol A. 2015. *African Realism? International Relations Theory and Africa's Wars in the Postcolonial Era*. Lanham, MD and London: Rowman and Littlefield.

Herbst, Jeffrey. 2000. *States and Power in Africa: Comparative Lessons in Authority and Control*. Princeton, NJ: Princeton University Press.

Huntington, Samuel P. 1996. *The Clash of Civilizations and the Remaking of World Order*. New York: Touchstone.

Hyden, Goran. 2013. *African Politics in Comparative Perspective*, 2nd ed. New York: Cambridge University Press.

Ibhawoh, Bonny and Akinosho, Lekan. 2018. 'Autocrats and Activists: Human Rights, Democracy and the Neoliberal Paradox in Nigeria', in Nana Poku and Jim Whitman (eds.), *Africa under Neoliberalism*. London and New York: Routledge, pp. 136–150.

Jackson, Richard. 2018. 'Post-Liberal Peace-Building and the Pacifist State', *Peacebuilding*, vol. 6, no. 1, pp. 1–16.

Jarstad, Anna K. and Belloni, Roberto. 2012. 'Introducing Hybrid Governance: Impact and Prospect of Liberal Peace-Building', *Global Governance*, vol. 18, no. 1, pp. 1–6.

Kingsbury, Damien. 2019. *Politics in Developing Countries*. London and New York: Routledge.

Knapp, Andrew and Footitt, Hilary. 2013. 'Introduction', in Andrew Knapp and Hilary Footitt (eds.), *Liberal Democracies at War: Conflict and Representation*. London, New Delhi, New York and Sydney: Bloomsbury, pp. 1–12.

Lazzarato, Mauricio. 2015. 'Neoliberalism, the Financial Crisis and the End of the Liberal State', *Theory, Culture and Society*, vol. 37, no. 7–8, pp. 67–83.

Little, Peter D. 2008. 'Comment: Reflection on Neo-Liberalism in Africa', *Focaal: European Journal of Anthropology*, vol. 51, pp. 148–150.

Mac Ginty, Roger. 2008. 'Indigenous Peace-Making versus the Liberal Peace', *Cooperation and Conflict: Journal of the Nordic International Studies Association*, vol. 43, no. 2, pp. 139–163.

Maines, David R. 1977. 'Social Organization and Social Structure in Symbolic Interactionist Thought', *Annual Review of Sociology*, vol. 3, pp. 235–259.

Menkhaus, Ken. 2012. 'After the Kenyan Intervention in Somalia', *Enough*. https://enoughproject.org/files/MenkhausKenyaninterventionSomalia.pdf. Accessed on 25 September 2019.

Mitchell, William and Fazi, Thomas. 2017. *Reclaiming the State: A Progressive Vision of Sovereignty for a Post-Neoliberal World*. London: Pluto Press.

Newman, Edward, Paris, Roland and Richmond, Oliver P. 2009. 'Introduction', in Edward Newman, Roland Paris and Oliver P. Richmond (eds.), *New Perspectives on Liberal Peace-Building*. Tokyo and New York: United Nations University Press, pp. 3–25.

Ngongo, Francis Kapalo. 2012. *Impasse of Post-Conflict Reconstruction: Economic Growth vs. Governance in Angola*. Houston, TX: Strategic Book Publishing and Rights Co.

Omach, Paul. 2012. 'The Limits of Disarmament, Demobilisation and Reintegration', in Devon Curtis and Gwinyayi Dzinesa (eds.), *Peace-Building, Power, and Politics in Africa*. Athens: Ohio University Press, pp. 87–104.

Paffenholz, Thania. 2015. 'Unpacking the Local Turn in Peacebuilding: A Critical Assessment towards an Agenda for Future Research', *Third World Quarterly*, vol. 36, no. 5, pp. 857–874.

Paris, Roland. 2010. 'Saving Liberal Peacebuilding', *Review of International Studies*, vol. 36, pp. 337–365.

Paris, Roland. 2002. 'International Peace-Building and the *Mission Civilisatrice*', *Review of International Studies*, vol. 28, no. 4, pp. 637–656.

Paris, Roland. 1997. 'Peace-Building and the Limits of Liberal Internationalism', *International Security*, vol. 22, no. 2, pp. 54–89.

Poku, Nana and Whitman, Jim (eds.). 2018. *Africa under Neoliberalism*. London and New York: Routledge.

Pureza, Jose Manuel. 2006. 'Three Deconstructions', in Jose Manuel Pureza et al., 'Peace-Building and Failed States: Some Theoretical Notes', *Oficina do CES* no. 256.

Reiter, Dan and Stam, Allan C. 2002. *Democracies at War*. Princeton, NJ and Oxford: Princeton University Press.

Reppell, Lisa, Rozen, Jonathan and Carvalho, Gustavo de. 2016. 'Planning for Peace: Lessons from Mozambique's Peacebuilding Process', *Institute for Security Studies*, ISS Paper 291/June 2016.

Richmond, Oliver P. 2013. 'The Legacy of State Formation Theory for Peacebuilding and Statebuilding', *International Peacekeeping*, vol. 20, no. 3, pp. 299–315.

Richmond, Oliver P. 2006. 'The Problem of Peace: Understanding the "Liberal Peace"', *Conflict, Security and Development*, vol. 6, no. 3, pp. 291–314.

Sabaratnam, Meera. 2011. 'Situated Critiques of Intervention: Mozambique and the Diverse Politics of Response', in Susanna Campbell, David Chandler and Meera Sabaratnam (eds.), *A Liberal Peace? The Problems and Practices of Peacebuilding.* London: Zed Books, pp. 245–264.

Sandbrook, Richard. 2007. 'Alternatives to Neo-Liberalism in the Third World', *Renewal*, vol. 15, nos. 2–3, pp. 46–57.

Serpe, Richard T. and Stryker, Shelden. 2011. 'The Symbolic Interactionist Perspective and Identity Theory', in Seth J. Schwartz, Koen Luyckx and Vivian L. Vignoles (eds.), *Handbook of Identity Theory and Research.* New York: Springer, pp. 225–248.

Shittu, Raji. 2015. 'Africa and the Philosophy of the New Partnership for Africa's Development (NEPAD)', *Journal of African Foreign Affairs,* vol. 2, nos. 1–2, pp. 27–48.

Swatuk, Larry A. 2018. 'Water, Water Everywhere but Not a Drop to Drink (Except for a Price)', in Nana Poku and Jim Whitman (eds.), *Africa under Neoliberalism.* London and New York: Routledge, pp. 115–135.

Tanabe, Juichiro. 2017. 'Beyond Liberal Peacebuilding: A Critique of Liberal Peacebuilding and Exploring a Modern Post-Liberal Hybrid Model of Peacebuilding', *International Relations and Diplomacy*, vol. 5, no. 8, pp. 447–459.

Thiessen, Charles. 2011. 'Emancipatory Peace-Building: Critical Response to (Neo)Liberal Trends', in Thomas Matyok, Jessica Senehi and Sean Byrne (eds.), *Critical Issues in Peace and Conflict Studies: Theory, Practice, and Pedagogy.* Lanham, MD and Plymouth: Lexington Books, pp. 115–140.

Thompson, Michael J. 2005. 'The World According to David Harvey', *Democratiya*, vol. 3, pp. 22–27.

Tom, Patrick. 2017. *Liberal Peace and Post-Conflict Peace-Building in Africa.* London: Palgrave Macmillan.

Trauschweizer, Ingo. 2014. 'Introduction', in Ingo Trauschweizer and Steven M. Miner (eds.), *Failed States and Fragile Societies: A New World Order?* Athens: Ohio University Press, pp. vii–xvii.

Tutuianu, Simona. 2013. *Towards Global Justice: Sovereignty in an Interdependent World.* The Hague: Asser Press.

Viterbo, Annamaria. 2018. 'The Role of the International Financial Institutions in Fragile and Conflict-Affected Countries', in Giovanni Cellamare and Ivan Ingravallo (eds.), *Peace Maintenance in Africa: Open Legal Issues.* Cham: Springer, pp. 111–134.

Wambugu, Nyambura. 2019. *Post-Conflict Security in South Sudan: From Liberal Peacebuilding to Demilitarization.* London, New York, Oxford, New Delhi and Sydney: I.B. Tauris.

Wiegratz, Jörg, Martiniello, Giuliano and Greco, Elisa. 2018. 'Introduction: Interpreting Changes in Neoliberal Uganda', in Jörg Wiegratz, Giuliano Martiniello and Elisa Greco (eds.), *Uganda: The Dynamics of Neoliberal Transformation.* London: Zed Books, pp. 1–40.

Wiley, Norbert C. 2003. 'The Self as Self-fulfilling Prophecy', *Symbolic Interaction*, vol. 26, no. 4, pp. 501–513.

Young, John. 2012. *The Fate of Sudan: The Origins and Consequences of a Flawed Peace Process.* London and New York: Zed Books.

3 Popular progressive peacebuilding and statebuilding

Introduction

I now examine an alternative to the neoliberal peacebuilding and statebuilding (PBSB) model discussed in the preceding chapter. This alternative is the popular progressive model. A critical question that informs this chapter is why we need an alternative model and what the foundations of the model are. In other words, how does the popular progressive differ from the neoliberal model? This question could be answered in several different ways. One answer would be because the neoliberal model has failed in bringing lasting and functional PBSB. Another would be because the neoliberal model is an alien imposition that goes against domestic endeavours and processes. Moreover, as an alien imposition mechanism, it ignores, undermines, devalues and downgrades local institutions, traditions, authorities, mechanisms and initiatives; and we know how colonialism relegated pre-colonial formal institutions and rule systems to informal status (Englebert, 2000; Kaplan, 2009; Sklar, 2005). A third answer, perhaps, would be because it is an elitist device that disempowers and disenfranchises the overwhelming majority of people, particularly, the rural population. One way or the other, the neoliberal approach has failed to generate peace, security, stability and development.

The most important characteristic that distinguishes the popular progressive model from the neoliberal is that it concerns fundamental societal construction, in a technical academic parlance nation and state formation. Therefore, the significance of the popular progressive peacebuilding approach is that it relates to a long-term evolutionary development of peace, because it addresses basic societal construction. The foundations of lasting peace and peacebuilding are deeply embedded in the foundations of societal construction. Peace, in this conception, is historical, contemporary and future oriented. It straddles the past–present–future continuum of birth, formation, transformation and maturity. It reflects the basic tenet that the past is in the present and the present is in the future. Societal construction is achieved in a protracted historical trajectory and continuum reflected in its ups and downs. In this sense, it would not be helpful to dissect the temporal continuum. Furthermore, in a broad and fundamental way, it is concerned with the profound project of gradual and evolutionary nation and state formation. In this sense, it is the antithesis of neoliberal quick fix PBSB. Basically, popular progressive PBSB deals with the evolutionary construction and reconstruction of society. The concepts of popular and progressive denote the dialectics between popular and progress. The 'popular' expresses the people-centred nature of PBSB, while 'progressive' connotes the long-term and continuous, future-oriented nature of PBSB that underscores justice, equality and egalitarianism. Understood in this way, PBSB constitutes an integral part of the fundamentals of societal construction in an evolutionary and progressive manner. Statebuilding, perceived as institutions-building, promotes peacebuilding. In other words, PBSB is a dialectics of two processes that essentially presuppose each other and whose metamorphosis grows from internal imperatives. While statebuilding and peacebuilding in the neoliberal model may (at least at the initial stage) be in conflict, in the popular progressive model, the one is a prerequisite for the other, and this is expressed in the intimately connected process of state emancipation and societal pacification that takes place over time and in a transformative process.

The point of departure of this chapter is that the popular progressive model is superior to the neoliberal version with regard to producing permanent PBSB. This is so because it prioritises the internal (what some call local) rather than the external (international). The internal or local is preferred not because it is free from complexity, difference of interests, inequality, differential power allocation among various sectors of society, but because it invites negotiations, dialogue, compromises, conciliations, give and take, consensus, etc. that are fundamental requisites for the condition of the will to live together among all the nation's stakeholders in an inclusive manner. You can do that only with members of society not with international actors. Internal dialogue, negotiations, compromises and inclusivity are core foundations of popular progressive PBSB that distinguish it from neoliberal. Unlike those who advocate hybrid between the local and international, popular progressive PBSB is perceived as dealing with the fundamentals of societal construction, thus a priority of the locals. Nevertheless, there are several dimensions that need to be taken into consideration, in order for the popular progressive PBSB to achieve its historical objectives. This chapter seeks to highlight those dimensions. In what follows, I analyse popular progressive peacebuilding and then popular progressive statebuilding. The next section deals with participatory democratic PBSB. After that there is an examination of the bottom-up and top-down strategy of PBSB. Finally, there are some conclusions.

Popular progressive peacebuilding

Johan Galtung's seminal work on peace, where he draws a distinction between positive and negative peace, has dominated the discourse on peace ever since it was introduced in 1964 (Grewal, 2003). Galtung introduced his peace conception as follows: 'there are two aspects of peace as conceived of here: *negative peace* which is the absence of violence, absence of war – and *positive peace* which is the integration of human society' (Galtung, 1964: 2, italics in original). The concept of positive peace is further elaborated to offer a broader definition of personal and structural peace. While personal peace refers to direct act of violence, structural peace has to do with indirect acts of violence; hence, the taxonomy of personal–structural and direct–indirect, or differently stated: personal–direct and structural–indirect (Galtung, 1969). The taxonomy constitutes Galtung's widely referenced conceptualisation of peace and peacebuilding.

Galtung's positive peace – perceived as the integration of human society – is closer to the popular progressive model advanced in this book. The validation of this interpretation would be clearly evidenced when we take note of Galtung's connotation of positive peace as social justice. The conceptualisation of social justice as the absence of social inequality and the construction of an egalitarian society would not only be more conducive to a peaceful society, but also a prerequisite for it. The evolution of an egalitarian society is predicated on the eradication of (or decrease in) structural violence, whose source is structural inequality. Galtung notes:

> whereas the absence of structural violence is what we have referred to as social justice, which is a positively defined condition (egalitarian distribution of power and resources). Thus peace conceived this way is not only a matter of control and reduction of the overt use of violence, but of what we have elsewhere referred to as 'vertical development'.
>
> (Galtung, 1969: 183)

The mention of vertical development is of great significance in Galtung's conceptualisation of positive peace, because it connects positive peace with development. He contends, without genuine development, there will not be positive peace, thus, Galtung further explains,

> peace research defined as research into the conditions – past, present and future – of realizing peace, will be equally intimately connected with conflict research and development research; the former often more relevant for negative peace and the latter more relevant for positive peace, but with highly important overlap'.
>
> (Galtung, 1969: 183)

In this conceptualisation, development is intimately associated with positive peace. Socio-economic development leading to abundance, and guided by equitable distribution, engenders egalitarianism and produces a peaceful society. This perception follows the tradition of classical economic liberalism and development sociology. The influential treatise on the wealth of nations (Adam Smith), for instance, predicted that the accumulation of wealth, accompanied by reasonably equitable distribution, would prevent class warfare and thereby lead to the pacification of society and the emergence of the welfare state. Development is a long process, as peacebuilding is. The accumulation of incremental economic wealth over prolonged timespan, dispersed among and benefiting citizens undergirds the conditions for positive peace, thus the peacebuilding-development nexus.

The basic premises of popular progressive peacebuilding are the embrace of holistic, national, regional, local ownership, indigenous institutions, authorities and mechanisms; inclusive bottom-up and top-down strategies (cf. Lederach, 1997; Mac Ginty, 2008; Richmond, 2011). The fundamental difference between the popular progressive model and reformist liberal peace (understood as neoliberal PBSB) with regard to top-down strategy, the former refers to top-down of the national state, not international actors. Other aspects of popular progressive peacebuilding include: local ownership of the agenda, process and solutions; long-term institution-building; complex negotiations, bargaining, compromise, reconciliation, participation, transformation; domestic process, home grown, no winner or loser outcome oriented, value systems and ethos. This could only be achieved within the frame of national stakeholders, interventionist international actorship would only play a disruptive role in this frame. According to Isaac O. Albert, peacebuilding in Africa rests on the 'commitment to cultural values, beliefs and norms of the people on the one hand and role expectation on the other' (Albert, 2008: 40). This confers legitimacy on the process (Jackson and Rosberg, 1984). Legitimacy is a cardinal prerequisite in any peacebuilding process. The generation of legitimacy rests on subject people owning and participating in values and norms that they recognise and revere, with interests and benefits that they draw on. Elite-based negotiations and dealings are the nemesis of popular progressive peacebuilding. Moreover, peaceful societal construction presupposes the cultivation of citizenry in and around idiosyncratic national values and norms. From a constructivist perspective, the citizenry is painstakingly moulded through the sociological process and mechanism of socialisation, internalisation and externalisation. This gains added significance in a societal setting that is poly-ethnic, poly-glottic and poly-religious, because the norms and values moulding the citizenry have to reflect the plurality of society. Hence, popular progressive peacebuilding has to construct from scratch the national norms and values necessary for sustainable and functional peacebuilding to take root. Stressing the socialisation of individuals within a specific cultural setting, and determinacy of knowledge, values and norms within that setting, Tanabe (2017: 452) notes, 'meaning of conflict, causes of conflict, meaning of peace, approaches to conflict resolution would be understood in different ways according to each culture'.

These are fundamental prerequisites for functional and sustainable peace. Peacebuilding in this perspective is exclusively domestic or home-grown (cf. Paffenholz, 2015). Any external involvement could only serve as an additional, supporting toolkit. Neoliberal peacebuilding is the antithesis of popular progressive peacebuilding, because its interventionist policies lead to state fragility, failure and collapse. While popular progressive focuses on elite-population, state-society constellation; neoliberal interventionism concern external actors-national elite constellation. Popular progressive peacebuilding endorses the view that 'actors are shaped by the socio-cultural milieu in which they live' (Conteh-Morgan, 2004: 234). In other words, it is culture and context contingent. To understand the coded and decoded means of communication, the facial, symbolic and verbal signals, requires in-depth *Verstehen* (interpretation), explanation and analysis that demand real cultural proficiency – which can only be attained by coming from within the common socio-cultural womb. Neoliberal socialisation in peacebuilding can only succeed in producing a small elite that is well oriented in it; an overwhelming majority of people are left out.

Popular progressive peacebuilding that is initiated in the wake of bloody war should aim at society-building. Society-building/reconstruction necessarily involves restoring destroyed values, norms, institutions, structures and relations (Curtis, 2012: 4–5). In other words, it craves the restoration of societal equilibrium, which derives from societal morality, values, norms and ethics. One of the consequences of war is the destruction of morality, values, institutions and trust – even the loss of humanity, as people in wartime may demonstrate brutal cruelty against their fellow human beings (Mamdani, 2009); therefore the main post-war peacebuilding responsibility would be to restore the balance and equilibrium lost. Society-building/reconstruction could not rest on borrowed values and norms (as in neoliberalism). The state of anomaly brought about by war must be replaced by a state of normality; only then can sustainable and functional peacebuilding be ensured (Tom, 2017). Grassroots-based peacebuilding would celebrate and reconstruct societal structures, norms and values that are communal, collectivist, solidarist and empathic (Conteh-Morgan, 2004; Gawerc, 2006).

Methodological collectivism, rather than methodological individualism, is the imperative of peacebuilding in the popular progressive alternative. It aims at restoring the balance, the equilibrium. 'Among African societies, symbols and rituals are key to an effective and permanent peacebuilding/reconstruction process' (Conteh-Morgan, 2004: 241). Restoration of the symbols and rituals damaged by war and conflict would rehabilitate the equilibrium. Characteristic features of popular progressive peacebuilding are engagement in a protracted discussion until consensus is reached among all citizens. The social fabric of peace rests on the moral authority and wisdom of elders, whose guidance, oversight, decisions and leadership – backed up by tried-and-tested praxis and ethos – are accepted and followed (Bereketeab, 2012). These are the moral threads that bind together citizens generating a functioning society. This is what was successively eroded during colonial and post-colonial periods, and during times of war. Mediations and verdicts handed down by elders are binding and implemented to the full. The reason they are accepted and obeyed is because they strive to restore social cohesion, harmony and equilibrium; not to punish, isolate and marginalise the guilty. Guilt is not an individual act, but is rather collective; and punishment and reward are also collective acts that aim to be restorative (Tom, 2017: 78–82). This is truly so because African societies are socio-centric, unlike Western which are ego-centric.

It should not, of course, be understood that the role of elders, chiefs or tradition is free from problems. To the contrary, it is full of shortcomings. But, the shortcomings are their own, therefore, familiarity, predictability and consistency that ease dealing with them. The significance of it in societal construction is it may serve as a repository of the past, norms, values and ethos that is lost on the young generation and could serve to restore balance and equilibrium thereby generating harmony, compromises and consensus. Moreover, as a repository of past experience and context, it serves as a toolkit from where to select the useful and discard the useless, thereby bettering the present and the future. This methodological collectivism in addressing disputes and offences, where extended families are involved both in taking responsibility for actions, and in undertaking reparations and restorations, ensures the sustainability of solutions, because it stands on solid foundations. Meanwhile methodological individualism, which hinges on individual punishment and individual reward, is profoundly precarious, because it is built on weak foundations. It lacks moral foundations, because the settlement of conflicts was based on pecuniary rewards and punishment.

The focus in the popular progressive peacebuilding model is on restorative, rather than retributive, peace. In this focus, the cultural resources of peace-making are of great significance (Conteh-Morgan, 2004). Familial connections, community networks, trust, dignity, integrity and respect are variables that create cohesion. These properties strongly contribute to the success of conflict mediation and ensure that people abide by the verdicts handed down by mediators. Both the mediators and the mediated are required to show impeccable social and moral integrity, otherwise they lose face in the community. Their wisdom and the respect they command within the community render elders the best possible institution to mediate, oversee, pass judgement and ensure that the decisions are implemented and heeded. The very fact that the elders possess only moral authority, integrity, selflessness and virtue secures obedience and respect (Bereketeab, 2012).

Throughout precolonial Africa, with a degree of variation, of course, it was a common phenomenon that the village community gathered together under a tree (still they do it in some places), under the aegis of elders, chief, council and discuss issues that concern them, an exercise of direct democracy, and would pass decisions through democratic consensus. Certainly, the village council excluded certain groups, but the democratic nature of decision-making overweighed the exclusion. Power of chiefs was curbed by popular will.

> consensus over substantive decisions was a central feature in most traditional African political system allowing rulers to exercise power and authority via some form of consultation with the

people. As Fortes and Evans-Pritchard point out, the 'structure of African State implies that kings and chiefs ruled by consent. A ruler's subjects are as fully aware of the duties he owes to them as they are of duties they owe to him, and are able to exert pressure to make him discharge the duties'.

(Tom, 2017: 18)

Colonialism undermined the direct democracy of precolonial communal Africa. The post-colonial Africa emerged as constituent of two asymmetrical spheres. The urban sphere, as the dominant, subordinated the rural sphere engendering constant conflicts and tensions. Those post-colonial states that were able to bridge the gap or strike a balance between the two spheres fared better in creating peace, stability and development. The case of Botswana and Somaliland as an illustration of hybrid is often raised. Both countries have done well in peacebuilding, stability, development and democratisation. A factor that is believed to have contributed to the creation of a hybrid system is British colonialism did not completely obliterate traditional structures, institutions and authorities in Botswana and Somaliland (Lewis, 2008; Peters, 1994; Samatar, 1997).

The micro-level (community) may, of course, differ from the macro-level (national) in terms of PBSB. Nation-building is invariably perceived as macro-level elite construction. The popular progressive model of nation-building, on the other hand, takes its point of departure as both micro-level bottom-up and macro-level top-down. While the bottom-up approach involves the participation of communities, the top-down approach represents the role of the elite, the two composite elements of the post-colonial state. To ensure peacebuilding, any successful nation-building has to combine the two levels. The methodology for translating the micro-level into the macro-level, and for bringing the macro-level closer to the micro-level, is the fundamental challenge that peacebuilding in Africa must grapple with. Because this is the very quintessential challenge that Africa is grappling with in its nation-building project. The conflicts, wars, insecurities and instabilities are related to the unfulfilled project of nation-building. Nation-building in Africa consists of the cultural construct (community) and the political construct (nation). It is a combination of ethnic and civic identities and modalities, which define and explain nation formation in the multi-ethnic societies of Africa (Bereketeab, 2011).

It is in this African context and reality that the neoliberal approach to African peacebuilding is heavily criticised. No wonder, then, that the neoliberal [liberal] peacebuilding model 'may be socially atomizing, hegemonic and lead to the valorization of a predatory state elite who gain easy access to an international economic and political cartography' (Oliver P. Richmond, quoted in Curtis, 2012: 16). Seen in this light, therefore, neoliberal peacebuilding runs counter to the aggregating, egalitarian and collective African values and norms (Ake, 2000). These are the values and norms that reinforce the functional and sustainable peace and peacebuilding that communities reach by engaging in continuous meetings until they iron out their differences. Whole villages sitting under trees for weeks on end to reach consensus – that was the usual mechanism of peacebuilding.

Moreover, being state centred, neoliberal peacebuilding is confined to global and national state levels, and thus is elitist and minoritarian, catering the urban minority elite. This ignores the sub-national, the marginalised, the peripheries, the indigenous, the traditional and the cultural context of common people. This is why it fails to foster lasting peace. Popular progressive peacebuilding, on the other hand, is people centred, pervasively inclusive, and straddles all the social ladders needed for success. The central concern in this approach is societal construction, which encompasses all citizens. This makes it a complex, protracted and sensitive political process, but at the same time functional and sustainable. The inclusivity is not, however, absolute: there are usually groups at the margin, for whatever reason. The most significant characteristics is, however, it make serious efforts to strike a balance between the two legacies to ensure sustainable and functional peacebuilding that is based on domestic reality. The following section analyses popular progressive statebuilding.

Popular progressive statebuilding

Gaining independence from colonialism was coveted as the prerequisite for popular progressive statebuilding in post-colonial Africa. The independence of erstwhile colonial societies, particularly in Africa, was expected to pave the way for the reconfiguration of these societies. The reconfiguration would follow the new societal edifice and legacy of the precolonial and colonial era. Therefore, it is noted, 'THE DREAMS OF INDEPENDENCE were scintillating. The young and ambitious generation of founding fathers articulated visions of negritude, African socialism, and pan-Africanism, all of which pointed from an oppressed past to a glorious future' (Christensen and Laitin, 2019: 31, emphasis in original). This was the spirit and letter of the epistemic and philosophical principle that guided the pioneer post-colonial leaders, who aspired to restore the dignity, integrity, virtue, rights and development of the people of the continent who were throwing off the yoke of servitude. Statebuilding founded on African values, norms, culture, civilisation, institutions, moral and ethos would negate and dislocate what colonialism had grafted onto the African social and political body. It was to stress this that Nkrumah coined his famous advice: 'Seek ye first the political kingdom and all else shall be added unto you' (Biney, 2011: 3). Once the emergent Africa gained the political kingdom, it could envision a bright future ahead of it. The post-colonial optimism also underpinned modernisation theory's jubilant prediction of successful nation statebuilding in Africa (modernisation theory was emerging as a dominant discourse at just that time). This powerful and infectious wind of hope and grandiose ambition of post-colonial nationalist elites to reconstruct their societies was reverberated across colonial societies, world over.

Statebuilding – a political endeavour *par excellence* – was seen as the very basic undertaking for dealing with all the pathologies afflicting Africa. The primary task the pioneer nationalist leaders set for themselves was two-pronged: deconstruction and construction. Deconstruction was concerned with dismantling structures, institutions, relations, etc. inherited from colonial times; construction involved building new structures, institutions, relations, etc. Unfortunately, many of the colonial structures, institutions, mechanisms, etc. were replicated (Ake, 2000; First, 1983; Tom, 2017), even though the nationalist leaders' intentions were different (Mamdani, 2017).

The noble project of constructing representative African states was, however, hijacked by internal and external forces. Internal hijacking occurred as a result of deviation of the post-colonial leaders from the solemn and noble dreams, visions and idealism they had initially displayed and promised (Ake, 2000). The optimism was replaced by identity conflicts, civil wars, military takeovers, one-party rule, poor governance, poverty, underdevelopment, etc. (Christensen and Laitin, 2019). Meanwhile, external hijacking began to plague the continent, when the erstwhile colonial powers shifted gear and embarked on perpetuating their domination and intervention, now using new forms and devices. Neo-colonialism and the Cold War, then the war on terror and the scramble for resources – one after the other these became the new devices to perpetuate domination (Schmidt, 2013; Tom, 2017; Yordanov, 2017). Writing about the neo-colonialism that replaced colonialism, Kwame Nkrumah (1970: ix) noted: 'The essence of neo-colonialism is that the State which is subject to it is, in theory, independent and has all the outward trapping of international sovereignty. In reality its economic system and thus its political is directed from outside.' Thus, the political economy of post-colonial statebuilding was controlled by the erstwhile masters.

Not only were Africans not given the time and opportunity to heal the wounds inflicted by colonialism, but also they were subjected to fresh wounds inflicted by new means. When Western college students (or others) react to courses that deal with the legacy of colonialism by saying that colonialism belongs to the past and Africans should shoulder responsibility for the problems besetting them, they not only forget the lasting structural deformation wrought on African societies by colonialism, but also fail to acknowledge the continuation of this practice by another means.

Peacebuilding and statebuilding in the popular progressive model are not only intimately connected, but also presuppose one another. As a presupposition to PBSB, the popular progressive model may entail a broader and longer duration. The state as both war-maker and peace-maker plays a pivotal role also in peacebuilding:

> Statebuilding in a strict sense is about creating the Weberian monopoly of legitimate violence over a defined territory, and therefore has at its core the concentration of the means of coercion in practical terms, armies and police – under the control of the central political authority. Both the liberal rule of law and democracy, by contrast involve *limiting* the central state's authority to coerce, the first by putting it under a set of transparent and universal rules, the second by ensuring that the exercise of power reflects the popular will.
>
> (Fukuyama, 2007: 11)

The allusion to monopoly of legitimate violence is associated with pacification of society (discussed in detail in the next chapter). The state as war-maker, as well as peace-maker, shoulders the responsibility for generating peace and engendering peacebuilding. As is noted above, two intimately connected processes and developments are vital in the state's cardinal function and prerequisite for peacebuilding: societal pacification and state emancipation. As functions of PBSB, these processes and developments quintessentially entail a protracted process. This is because statebuilding is institution-building – and building institutions is time-consuming. In addition, once built the institutions need routinisation, bureaucratisation, predictability and dependability. In other words, they have to constitute a culture where citizens will not only be able to recognise them easily, but will also own them, abide by them, respect and adore them. For these characteristics to develop, the institutions should reflect and be the repository for local norms, values, belief systems, social and cultural structures. They should tell of local heroes, sagas, shrines, valleys, mountains, seas, skies, etc. In other words, they should reflect the day-to-day life of citizens.

Moreover, popular progressive statebuilding is characterised by two defining features. The first is, statebuilding, by its very nature is a domestic process. As such therefore, it should involve negotiations, bargains, compromises, conciliations, dialogue, participation, etc. of all societal stakeholders. These stakeholders may represent class, social groups, gender, ethnicity, religion, generation, region, mode of life. In a pluralistic societal setting only such inclusive, representative mechanism could achieve a functional, sustainable and democratic statebuilding. The second feature is statebuilding is political by nature. Politics is about power, and power is expressed in who takes what, when and how. The neoliberal allocation of power based on electoral winner takes all have failed to bring peace, stability, unity and development in Africa. Democratic statebuilding that fails to take into serious consideration the societal setting of African societies is doomed to fail. Above all, statebuilding, in the popular progressive model, should strive to reconcile and strike a balance between the two publics that were engendered by colonialism and defining post-colonial Africa.

Another significant feature of popular progressive statebuilding is it consists of both bottom-up and top-down methodological strategy. This strategy helps to reconcile the binary cleavage created by colonialism. Post-colonial African societies embody what Ekeh (1975) call two publics and Mamdani (2017) designated despotic decentralisation. The two are the urban-centres, Western-oriented elite-dominated public and the overwhelming rural population. These are often pitted against one another as rivals. Post-colonial statebuilding in Africa is shattered by this rivalry. Therefore, the central objective of the popular progressive model is to reconcile the two realms of society. The top-down (national level), catering the urban sphere, and the bottom-up (local-community level) catering the rural sphere, are intended to bring them together in the alluded statebuilding process. State fragility, weakness, collapse, crisis certainly stems from the absence of reconciliation of the two. Basically, the urban, as representative of the state remains in suspension from the rural, representing society. A penetrative engagement of the two is necessary for prevalence of the functional representative state. In the African societal setting, paying due attention to the two levels is of decisive importance, making or breaking. In addition, it is important to take note of the complexity of the local level. When we talk about the local, in our perspective, we have to make sure we are talking about a multi-ethnic, multi-lingual, multi-religious, multi-cultural societal setting that demands a careful consideration. Inclusion, participation, recognition and acceptance, compromises of multiple national actors should be involved in the process, design and construction of the state.

The focus of popular progressive statebuilding is, therefore, to harness the properties underpinning statebuilding in Africa. There is no illusion that colonialism produced what Peter Ekeh (1975) has called two publics intricately tied together. Others have dubbed the development 'institutional duality' (Englebert, 2000; Sklar, 2005). One public represents the colonial heritage; the other – African heritage. The existence of the dichotomous publics and institutions in the African body politics therefore behoves actors to pay attention to hybridity and to striking a balance between them. In statebuilding under the popular progressive approach, the socialisation, internalisation and externalisation processes are there to make Africans conscious of their double heritage, and to get them to design and build their states based on their own norms and values. The next section analyses the form of democratic statebuilding conducive to the realities of developing societies.

Participatory democratic peacebuilding and statebuilding

The issue of democracy is another dimension that generates controversy in conjunction with PBSB. Historically, no connection used to be made between democracy and statebuilding (Mengisteab and Daddieh, 1999). Today, connecting democracy with statebuilding has become highly fashionable in the literature, thus the notion of democratic statebuilding (Edozie, 2009; Moradian, 2010; Tapscott et al., 2018). A critical question that deserves a response, however, is which version of democracy and democratisation? In recent years, democracy has simply been associated with neoliberal formalist and electoral form of democracy, particularly with reference to interventionist international PBSB. The post–Cold War era witnessed a marked increase in interventions in fragile conflict-ridden societies with the aim of statebuilding and peacebuilding. Fixing post-conflict fragile or collapsed societies in the neoliberal regime simply became reconfiguring the societies with Western values and norms. This in itself, instead of fixing the societies, exposed them to further maladies and fragilities. Is a neoliberal-driven democratisation process in developing and conflict-prone societies plausible?

Neoliberal discourse accepts only one strand of democracy, and prescribes the one-size-fits-all straitjacket solution. The evidence on the ground however does not corroborate to the suitability of the neoliberal one-size-fits-all straitjacket solution. The problems are complex with multiple root causes and require multiple approaches and solutions. It is possible to identify a range of problems that render the neoliberal version of democracy highly non-conducive and dysfunctional, for instance, in the African societal setting. One of these dysfunctionalities is its elitist nature. Neoliberal democracy is predicated on formal, competitive, frequently recurring elections to choose between elite groups that succeed one another in assuming state power. Classical theories of democracy identify at least three types: direct or plebiscitary (Jean Jacques Rousseau); representative or liberal (John Stuart Mill, James Madison, John Locke); and pluralist (Joseph Schumpeter, Robert Dahl). These types correspond to: decision by all citizens; decision by accountable leaders; and competition between elites, respectively (cf. Held, 1987). The first type, direct or plebiscitary, is generally connected with small village or town communities. Therefore, its applicability to modern large-scale societies is put into question. And so the two others compete for relevance in serving Western societies. Although Western democracies credit themselves with being representative and liberal, critics point out that Western democracies are simply an exercise in competition between elites. The pluralist approach – sometimes also known as Schumpeterian – both in theory and practice represents a narrow conceptualisation and application of democracy. Schumpeter opined, 'the people have the opportunity of accepting or refusing the men who are to rule them' via 'competitive elections' (Selinger, 2015: 127). This minimalist conception of democracy may be now the driving force of neoliberalism. Some define the minimalist or procedural as, 'fully contested elections with full suffrage and the absence of massive fraud, combined with effective guarantees of civil liberties, including freedom of speech, assembly, and association' (Collier and Levitsky, 1997: 434).

The three types of democracy are an outcome of historical, cultural, socio-economic, political and philosophical development and transformation in the West. This evolutionary transformation was accompanied by a corresponding transformation featuring the individualisation, secularisation, industrialisation and urbanisation of societies. Indeed, it is an outcome of what Anthony D. Smith (1986) designated the triple Western revolution: administrative and military; economic; and cultural and educational. In this sense, they are time, culture and space specific. As such, would it then be possible to simply transfer them to some other time, culture and space-specific setting?

The question we need to pose is, then, will a narrow and procedural understanding and method of exchanging power among elites serve societies in Africa well? Moreover, would PBSB based on these premises produce enduring and functional peace and states? Neoliberal-informed democratisation uses as a benchmark whether a number of consecutive elections has taken place, how many political parties competed, how free the electoral competition was, what the role of the media was (was it free), how the electoral law is framed, how the participation of civil society was, whether it allows external observers, etc. (Bratton and de Walle, 1997). But does this technical and procedural form of democracy really address the needs of the overwhelming majority of society, particularly the rural population? Those who are served by the technical and procedural form are the minority urban and literate population (Ake, 2000). Meanwhile, the overwhelming majority – in particular, the rural population, women and youth – are isolated and marginalised. In addition, in a multicultural, pluralist society, it leads to ethnic domination, by vesting power in one ethnic group. As post-colonial African history unequivocally testifies, military rule, one-party rule and one-man rule have alternated, including in countries where elections have taken place (Goulbourne, 1987). Even if an alternation of elites does take place, it does not prevent a descent into conflict, civil war, intra- and inter-communal, intra- and inter-state conflict. A good example is Kenya, although oriented towards Western democracy since independence, and conducts recurrent elections, yet is marred by violent conflicts (Kagwanja and Southall, 2009).

The outcome of all these pathologies has been abysmal poverty, unemployment, underdevelopment, inequality, socio-economic stagnation and degradation (Bereketeab, 2013). Above all, the statebuilding and nation-building project that was widely perceived as a prerequisite for peace, stability, unity, territorial integrity and development in the post-colonial period faltered (Ake, 2000). The post-colonial state simply became a continuation of its predecessor, the colonial state, thereby becoming a source of chronic conflicts. The chronic conflicts, in turn, adversely affected the process of post-colonial statebuilding. In other words, the nature of the state-generated conflicts and the conflicts dictated the statebuilding process. The notion of democratic statebuilding, under interventionist neoliberalism, is permeated with problems. The chief cause for this is that statebuilding, as institution-building, is based on replicating Western institutions.

The neoliberal mode of thinking of democratic statebuilding became dominant in the aftermath of the Cold War and overshadowed any other world overview. Earlier, it was common to draw a distinction between procedural democracy and substantive democracy (Collier and Levitsky, 1997; Kingsbury, 2019). In the 1970s and 1980s, the democratic discourse was characterised by at least two versions of democracy and democratisation with regard to developing societies. Many progressive scholars, realising the shortcomings of the neoliberal conception of democracy and democratisation in relation to Africa, strongly leaned towards the substantive version. One of the central tenets of substantive democracy and democratisation is participatory democracy. Unlike neoliberal procedural democracy, participatory democracy tends to be popular and inclusive, in the sense that common people are allowed the space to shape national politics and governance matters. Substantive democracy focuses on quality: it strives to provide an answer to the question how does democracy improve the quality of life of the common people? The central focus of substantive or participatory democracy is considered to be improving the quality of life. It is argued that the improvement can only be achieved through the genuine empowerment of citizens. Genuine empowerment, in turn, can only be achieved through genuine participation, not through elite representation. The participation of citizens in political, economic, cultural, social and governance matters would ensure the kind of substantive democracy that could change their lives.

> Unlike liberal democracy, the popular conception of democracy does not limit the practice of democracy to the political sphere alone but rather expands democracy's meaning to include how a society's resources are used and distributed. The salience of populist genres of democratic expression in Africa is explained by the continued limitation that the incumbent liberal democracies are having in providing economic and social welfare benefits to underdeveloped and unevenly developed African Societies.
>
> (Edozie, 2009: 29)

Participatory democracy is the antithesis of neoliberal democracy in a number of respects. First, instead of an elite, it is founded on common citizens and is people centred. Secondly, it pays due attention to indigenous norms, values, institutions, authorities and mechanisms. Most African societies in the pre-colonial period had local assemblies where village communities would deliberate – if necessary, for days – until they reached a consensus on economic, political, social, cultural, security or governance matters. An illustration of this is provided by the South African anthropologist, Isaac Schapera when he writes,

> all matter of tribal policy are dealt with finally before a general assembly of the adult males in the chief's *kgotla* (council place). Such meetings are very frequently held...among the topics discussed... are tribal disputes, quarrels between the chief and his relatives, the imposition of new levies, the undertaking of new public works, the promulgation of new decrees by the chief...it is not unknown for the tribal assembly to overrule the wishes of the chief. Since anyone may speak, these meetings enable him to ascertain the feelings of the people generally, and provide the latter with an opportunity of stating their grievances. If the occasion calls for it, he and his advisers may be taken severely to task, for the people are seldom afraid to speak openly and frankly.
>
> (quoted in Acemoglu and Robinson, 2013: 407)

This participatory democracy in the deliberation, accountability of office holder, and decision-making in matters that concern the community was a widely exercised political mechanism in pre-colonial Africa. Leaders were accountable to the people and severely punished by the people for misconduct or failure to fulfil their duties (Tom, 2017).

Some call this communocracy or village democracy (Edozie, 2009). This resembled direct or plebiscitary democracy, as elaborated by Rousseau. In direct democracy or participatory democracy, the majority are included. Most importantly, is not a zero-sum game of winners and losers. Consensus is the name of the game: in the old assemblies, they would discuss the matter in hand until everyone was brought on board. Thirdly, the moral authority of elders and of the councils was the real source of power. Moral authority was earned by impeccable integrity, neutrality and responsibility in discharging one's duties. There was no army, police, prison and law-enforcement agents or instruments of sanction. Decisions and verdicts were heeded and followed to the letter, out of respect for the elders and council members, and the customs, ethos and praxis guiding the community. This pre-colonial communocracy is believed to have existed in parts of Africa.

> This genre of democratic practice is found in many parts of traditional Africa. It has the ability to enhance popular participation in societal governance. Not only were household heads and adult males admitted in village councils and had effective voice

in deliberation in their individual and representative capacities, but there were also provisions for individuals who otherwise could not participate formally in decision making to air their views in village square public gatherings.

(Edozie, 2009: 31)

All this was eroded by the colonial and post-colonial state. The customs, ethos and praxis that used to be formal and governing institutions and tools in pre-colonial government and governance were downgraded to informality (Englebert, 2000; Sklar, 2005). They were replaced with colonial metropolitan laws and rules. This downgrading to informality then excluded the overwhelming majority, particularly the rural population, from state affairs. The few members of the urban elite were catered for by the colonially imposed Western laws and rules, while the rural majority stuck with their (now informal) customary law. This eventually produced two governance systems, rural and urban (Ekeh, 1975; Mamdani, 1996). It is this system of two parallel rules that the popular progressive model intends to bridge. Embedded in this model, participatory democracy and democratic statebuilding, in contrast to neoliberal democracy, would revive and resuscitate what has been transformed into informality. Elevating the informal to the formal would help to create a hybrid system of democracy and democratisation in Africa, in the spirit of popular progressive statebuilding and peacebuilding.

The formal version of democracy that is often associated with the liberal/neoliberal democracy that assumed dominance in the wake of the Cold War and that guided interventionist statebuilding and peacebuilding in post-conflict societies proved detrimental to peace, stability and development, not only in those societies but also worldwide. The target societies could not benefit from the intervention, because it was motivated by ideological persuasion, rather than founded on hard reality. In addition, it exposed the world to further conflicts, extremism, radicalism and fundamentalism, as witnessed in Afghanistan, Iraq, Somalia, Libya, Syria, Yemen, the Sahel, etc.

It is also of great significance to discern between democracy as a system and democratisation as a process. Systems are full-fledged edifices that encompass entirely and constitute a governance system of contemporary society. A system embodies culture, institutions, praxis, habits and ethos that give it predictability and accountability. A process on the other hand, is still an evolving, not yet fully grown, phenomenon. As such lacks form and predictability. African societies are not democratic systems, in the Western sense of the concept.

They find themselves in the process of democratisation. This confusion and failure to make the discernibility leads to wrong assessment and conclusion about Africa. One common wrong assumption is juxtaposing old Western societies (five hundred years old) with young Africa (sixty years old).

Bottom-up and top-down strategy of peacebuilding and statebuilding

There are two different strategies of peacebuilding and statebuilding: the bottom-up strategy and the top-down strategy. Sometimes these are deployed separately, depending on ideological orientation; at other times they are used in combination. Accordingly, they are deployed differently in the neoliberal model and the popular progressive model. Strategies of PBSB in the neoliberal model are as discussed often top-down. There are valid reasons for this. One could be ideological persuasion. In addition, PBSB, in neoliberalism, is accomplished through the involvement of international actors. External peace-builders and state-builders come with their own ideological baggage that runs counter to the reality on the ground. This is the belief that the elite possess the capacity or right to engender PBSB. Another could be constraints of resources and time: resources are always limited, particularly when they are not internally generated. As often is the case neoliberal PBSB is contingent on donor's generosity. These two factors would then compel the strategy option to be top-down. Perhaps a third reason could be that neoliberal interventionist statebuilding and peacebuilding tend to deal with societies under stress, embroiled in conflict or just emerging from conflict and war. Therefore, there is a sense of urgency (although hasty action may not yield the necessary outcome). In some neoliberal circles, the reformist one, we find attempts of conflation of top-down and bottom-up strategies of PBSB. Yet, responsibilities are allocated to different actors, local (national) and international. Referring to Richmond's (2011) work, Tanabe (2017: 454), states,

> Based on the deconstruction of binary thinking of either liberal or locally framed peace as the absolute answer for a lasting peace, the core of postmodern post-liberal hybrid peacebuilding is the recognition that both internal and external commitments are indispensable: International actors, local actors and constituencies cannot operate effectively without each other...It is a reframing of

peacebuilding as a dialogical process that reconstructs the every-day according to how its local subjects need and want to live in the broader liberal peace context, but also in recognition of multiple everydays and mutual engagements...It is an organic interconnec-tion between the international and local everyday.

This assumption is based on a hypothesis that those conflict-shattered 'need and want to live in the broader liberal peace context'. This is an assumption that could only be verified empirically. The second prob-lem with the assumption is the place and space given to the local (that is the marginalised social and ethnic groups and rural population). In poly-ethnic, poly-glottic, poly-religious and poly-cultural societies, the setting is complex and multiple national stakeholders are required to be involved.

The popular progressive approach distinguishes itself from the ne-oliberal. The distinction is that the popular progressive model should, of necessity and by choice, pursue a blend of bottom-up and top-down: *of necessity*, because post-colonial African societies are a merger of two legacies – the alien colonial transplantation, and the indigenous extension of the pre-colonial, generating, in Peter Ekeh's (1975) term 'two publics'. Post-colonial Africa is a hybrid of the pre-colonial (which resiliently survived the colonial onslaught and asserted itself in post-colonial times) and that which colonialism implanted. Hence, PBSB strategies need to be framed in a way that both legacies are prop-erly served. Hence, the top-down and bottom-up strategy of PBSB is a precluded zone. The preclusion refers to the perimeters of the national circle: micro-sociological level (local) and macro-sociological level (national). Since it is about societal construction, all societal groups should be involved and it is a task to be accomplished by them, thus, we say societal construction is by its very nature domestic.

The bottom-up approach may cater to the rural 'traditional' com-munity, often designated as informal, that was relegated from for-mal to informal by colonialism (Englebert, 2000; Sklar, 2005), while the top-down approach caters to the urban 'modern' public, which retained formality under colonialism and after. *By choice*, because awareness of the existence of the two publics induces the instinct that managing it may be better served by striking a balance between the two formations. In other words, accepting the duality spurs the choice of deploying bottom-up and top-down strategies. Somaliland is widely praised for its success in indigenous peacebuilding and state building (Jhazbhay, 2009; Walls, 2014). This success is attributed to the conflation of traditional and modern institutions, authorities and mechanism. Somaliland introduced the bicameral system: the upper house consisting of the house of elders, the Guurti, and the lower house, consisting of the elected parliament. The two institutions share constitutionally delineated and determined discretionary powers where they exercise sole powers in their respective areas of discretionary power. While the Guurti represents the clans (grassroots), the parliament represent the state. Bringing these two together is a good application of the strategy of bottom-up and top-down. This hybridity is presumed to have brought peace, stability and democracy to Somaliland, while neoliberal interventionism has failed in south Somalia.

A second case widely seen as a success showcasing the popular progressive PBSB model is Botswana. The formation of bicameral parliament where traditional authorities, notably the chiefs were accommodated in the post-colonial state structure provided the needed imputes for peace and stability. The House of Chiefs, in the bicameral parliamentary system conferred traditional authority and institution a say in the running of the country thereby affording the state the highly needed legitimacy (Samatar, 1997). This legitimacy, in turn, arguably afforded the system stability. An element that presumably facilitated the success story in both cases is that colonialism did not fundamental change the social structure, many of precolonial structures and institutions remained intact.

The two formations express a condition of hybridity – which, by definition, implies a system consisting of two legacies. The resulting species (hybrid) contains binary properties that require us, in our dealings with the hybrid, to balance the two inherent properties. The hybridity of the colonially produced societal formation compels us to employ the bottom-up and top-down methodological strategy in dealing with PBSB. The bottom-up strategy would serve, primarily, as a construction strategy that extends from the micro-level (community) to the macro-level (national). The top-down strategy, on the other hand, represents a declining order – from the macro level (national) to the micro level (community). The community-centred strategy would serve the overwhelmingly rural population, while the national-level strategy would serve the urban populace. The expediency of the methodological hybridity lies in the role it plays in bridging the cleavages that colonialism created – particularly rural/urban. It helps to connect the two publics, thereby contributing to an enduring and functioning PBSB on the principles of the popular progressive model. In a nutshell, reconciling and combining the two strategies would promote genuine statebuilding and peacebuilding in Africa.

Conclusion

The popular progressive PBSB model, proposed as an alternative to the neoliberal model, involves an analysis and examination of indigenous African institutions, structures, mechanisms, dynamics and realities. These are prerequisites for a sustainable and functional peace and state. In this manner, an understanding of the popular progressive model involves the basics of societal construction – in technical parlance, with nation and state formation. Construction of society is a necessary presupposition of peacebuilding as a long-term, strategic objective. The epistemic and ontological foundation of the popular progressive model rests, therefore, on a critique of neoliberalism. The chapter contends a serious critique that goes beyond simple reform is required. The popular progressive model is an attempt to interrogate and navigate the root causes of conflicts, state fragility and the consequent lack of peace, stability and development. It comes to the conclusion that the incomplete societal construction is due to the conflicts, fragility and related pathologies. Hence, the production of alternative and innovative knowledge, concepts and methodology is required to understand and foster popular progressive PBSB.

This chapter has sought to explore and develop an innovative model that is based on the reality of a society. The central point of departure of the chapter is that statebuilding and peacebuilding are, by their very nature, political and domestic. Therefore, they should be based on a society's specific realities. Moreover, they need to involve all stakeholders – and that requires engaging in genuine and protracted negotiations, bargaining, dialogue, compromise and prolonged sessions to reach consensus. Consensus, in turn, presupposes familiar, recognised and recognisable, tried, tested and trusted patterns, and common values and norms. Socialisation in the collective or community-based values and norms would ensure durable peacebuilding and functioning statebuilding, since the construction of common identity constitutes the cornerstone of societal formation. There is a need to take advantage of the dual role of the state – peace-making and war-making – and retune it to become a positive and constructive force for peace that embodies the common values and norms. Only a state that embodies common national values and norms can represent all communities; only then can citizens feel that the state belongs to them and that they own it. Only such a state can engender peace and engage in real peace-making rather than war-making. A state that is able to fulfil these objectives ought to be based on the popular progressive model. That model is an embodiment of the dual heritage of the African state.

Thus, it endeavours to reinstate equilibrium. Equilibrium could only be achieved through popular participation, inclusion, representation, recognition and acceptance of diversity and plurality. This, again, requires conciliation and striking a balance between cleavages. SBPB, in the popular progressive model, as domestic and political by their very nature, could only be achieved by the participation and inclusion of all societal stakeholders without external interference.

The cornerstone of the popular progressive perception is stakeholders should own the agenda, process and outcome of PBSB. Ownership implies designing, programming, controlling and effectuating on the basis of internal reality, context, balance of power, philosophy and ideology. This, however does not mean complete exclusion of external support. National stakeholder could consensually seek for material, technical and ideational support in a manner that allows them overall control without blatant intervention that disrupts societal balance. Citizens should be able to build their own house according to their needs and capacity. Only then could we have functioning, sustainable equitable PBSB.

References

Acemoglu, Daron and Robinson, James A. 2013. *Why Nations Fail: The Origin of Power, Prosperity and Poverty.* London: Profile Books LTD.

Ake, Claude. 2000. *The Feasibility of Democracy in Africa.* Dakar: Council for the Development of Social Science Research in Africa (CODESRIA).

Albert, Isaac O. 2008. 'Understanding Peace in Africa', in David J. Francis (ed.), *Peace and Conflict in Africa.* London: Zed Books, pp. 31–45.

Bereketeab, Redie (ed.). 2013. *The Horn of Africa: Intra-State and Inter-State Conflicts and Security.* London: Pluto Press.

Bereketeab, Redie. 2012. 'Re-Examining Local Governance in Eritrea: The Redrawing of Administration Regions', *African and Asian Studies*, vol. 11, nos. 1–2, pp. 1–29.

Bereketeab, Redie. 2011. 'Ethnic and Civic Foundation of Citizenship and Identity in the Horn of Africa', *Studies of Ethnicity and Nationalism*, vol. 11, no. 1, pp. 63–81.

Biney, Ama. 2011. *The Political and Social Thought of Kwame Nkrumah.* New York: Palgrave Macmillan.

Bratton, Michael and De Walle, Nicolas. 1997. *Democratic Experiment in Africa: Regime Transition in Comparative Perspective.* Cambridge: Cambridge University Press.

Christensen, Darin and Laitin, David D. 2019. *African States since Independence: Order, Development, and Democracy.* New Haven, CT and London: Yale University Press.

Collier, David and Levitsky, Steven. 1997. 'Democracy with Adjectives: Conceptual Innovation in Comparative Research', *World Politics*, vol. 49, pp. 430–451.

Conteh-Morgan, Earl. 2004. 'Peace-Building and Human Security: A Constructivist Perspective', in Hideaki Shinoda and Ho-Won Jeong (eds.), *Conflict and Human Security: A Research for New Approaches of Peace-Building*, IPSHU English Research Report Series No. 19. Hiroshima: Hiroshima University, pp. 229–251.

Curtis, Devon. 2012. 'The Contested Politics of Peace-Building in Africa', in Devon Curtis and Gwinyayi Dzinesa (eds.), *Peace-Building, Power, and Politics in Africa*. Athens: Ohio University Press, pp. 1–28.

Edozie, Rita Kiki. 2009. *Reconstructing the Third Wave of Democracy: Comparative African Democratic Politics*. Lanham, MD, Boulder, CO, New York, Toronto and Plymouth: University Press of America.

Ekeh, Peter P. 1975. 'Colonialism and the Two Publics in Africa: A Theoretical Statement', *Comparative Studies in Society and History*, vol. 17, no. 1, pp. 91–112.

Englebert, Pierre. 2000. *State Legitimacy and Development in Africa*. Boulder, CO: Lynne Rienner Publishers.

First, Ruth. 1983. 'Colonialism and the Formation of African States', in David Held et al. (eds.), *States and Societies*. Oxford and Cambridge, MA: Blackwell, pp. 207–218.

Fukuyama, Francis. 2007. 'Liberalism versus Statebuilding', *Journal of Democracy*, vol. 18, no. 3, pp. 10–13.

Galtung, Johan. 1969. 'Violence, Peace, and Peace Research', *Journal of Peace Research*, vol. 6, no. 3, pp. 167–191.

Galtung, Johan, 1964. 'An Editorial', *Journal of Peace Research*, vol. 1, no. 1, pp. 1–4.

Gawerc, Michelle I. 2006. 'Peacebuilding: Theoretical and Concrete Perspectives', *Peace and Change*, vol. 31, no. 4, pp. 435–478.

Goulbourne, Harry. 1987. 'The State, Development and the Need for Participatory Democracy in Africa', in Peter Anyang' Nyong'o (ed.), *Popular Struggles for Democracy in Africa*. London, New Jersey and Tokyo: Zed Books and the United Nations University, pp. 26–47.

Grewal, Baljit Singh. 2003. *Johan Galtung: Positive and Negative Peace*. School of Social Science: Auckland University of Technology.

Held, David. 1987. *Model of Democracy*. Cambridge: Polity Press.

Jackson, Robert and Rosberg, Carl G. 1984. 'Popular Legitimacy in African Multi-Ethnic States', *Journal of Modern African Studies*, vol. 22, no. 2, pp. 177–198.

Jhazbhay, Igbal. 2009. *Somaliland: An African Struggle for Nationhood and International Recognition*. Midrand and Johannesburg: The Institute for Global Dialogue and The South African Institute of International Affairs.

Kagwanja, Peter and Southall, Roger. 2009. 'Introduction: Kenya – A Democracy in Retreat', *Journal of Contemporary African Studies*, vol. 27, no. 3, pp. 259–277.

Kaplan, Seth. 2009. 'Rethinking State Building'. *The Broker*, 16 October.

Kingsbury, Damien. 2019. *Politics in Developing Countries*. London and New York: Routledge.

Lederach, John Paul. 1997. *Building Peace: Sustainable Reconciliation in Divided Societies*. Washington, DC: United States Institute of Peace.

Lewis, Ioan. 2008. *Understanding Somalia and Somaliland*. London: Hurst & Company.

Mac Ginty, Roger. 2008. 'Indigenous Peace-Making versus the Liberal Peace', *Cooperation and Conflict: Journal of the Nordic International Studies Association*, vol. 43, no. 2, pp. 139–163.

Mamdani, Mahmood. 2017. *Citizen and Subject: Contemporary Africa and the Legacy of Late Colonialism, with a New Preface*. Johannesburg and Kampala: Wits University Press and Makerere Institute of Social Research.

Mamdani, Mahmood. 2009. *Saviors and Survivors: Darfur, Politics, and the War on Terror*. New York and Toronto: Pantheon Books.

Mamdani, Mahmood. 1996. *Citizens and Subjects: Contemporary Africa and the Legacy of Late Colonialism*. Princeton, NJ: Princeton University Press.

Mengisteab, Kidane and Daddieh, Cyril. 1999. 'Why State Building Is Still Relevant in Africa and How It Relates to Democratization', in Kidane Mengisteab and Cyril Daddieh (eds.), *State Building and Democratization in Africa*. Westport, CT and London: Praeger, pp. 1–18.

Moradian, Davood. 2010. 'Democratic Statebuilding as an Effective and Enduring Conflict Resolution Strategy for Afghanistan', paper presented at Building the Security in Asia and CICA, Uluslarrasi Turk-Asy Kongresi/5th International Turkish-Asian Congress, 3–5 June, Cevahir Congress Center, Istanbul, Turkey.

Nkrumah, Kwame. 1970. *Neo-Colonialism: The Last Stage of Imperialism*. London: PANAF.

Paffenholz, Thania. 2015. 'Unpacking the Local Turn in Peace-Building: A Critical Assessment towards an Agenda for Future Research', *Third World Quarterly*, vol. 36, no. 5, pp. 857–874.

Peters, Pauline. 1994. *Dividing the Commons: Politics, Policy, and Culture in Botswana*. Charlottesville: Virginia University Press.

Richmond, Oliver P. 2011. 'Critical Agency, Resistance and Post-Colonial Civil Society', *Cooperation and Conflict*, vol. 46, no. 4, pp. 419–440.

Samatar, Abdi Ismail. 1997. 'Leadership and Ethnicity in the Making of African State Models: Botswana versus Somalia', *Third World Quarterly*, vol. 18, no. 4, pp. 687–708.

Schmidt, Elizabeth. 2013. *Foreign Intervention in Africa: From the Cold War to the War on Terror*. Cambridge: Cambridge University Press.

Selinger, William. 2015. 'Schumpeter on Democratic Survival', *The Tocqueville Review/La Revue Tocqueville*, vol. 36, no. 2, pp. 127–157.

Sklar, Richard L. 2005. 'The Premise of Mixed Government in African Political Studies', in Olufemi Vaughan (ed.), *Tradition and Politics: Indigenous Political Structure in Africa*. Trenton, NJ and Asmara: Africa World Press, pp. 13–32.

Smith, Anthony D. 1986. *The Ethnic Origins of Nations*. Oxford and Cambridge, MA: Blackwell.

Tanabe, Juichiro. 2017. 'Beyond Liberal Peacebuilding: A Critique of Liberal Peacebuilding and Exploring a Modern Post-Liberal Hybrid Model of Peace-building', *International Relations and Diplomacy*, vol. 5, no. 8, pp. 447–459.

Tapscott, Chris, Halvorsen, Tor, and Rosari, Teresita Cruz–del. 2018. *The Democratic Developmental State: North-South Perspective*. New York: Columbia University Press.

Tom, Patrick. 2017. *Liberal Peace and Post-Conflict Peace-Building in Africa*. London: Palgrave Macmillan.

Walls, Michael. 2014. *A Somali Nation-State: History, Culture and Somali-land's Political Transition*. Pisa: Ponte Invisible Edizioni, AREDSEA-ONLINE Publishing Group Company.

Yordanov, Radoslav A. 2017. The Soviet Union and the Horn of Africa during the Cold War: Between Ideology and Pragmatism. Lanham, MD, Boulder, CO, New York and London: Lexington Books.

4 State emancipation and societal pacification as prerequisites for peacebuilding

Introduction

It took several hundred years for the predecessor of the post-colonial Western state to emancipate itself, and pacification of the society under its control (Young, 1994: 15–16). Indeed, numerous wars – the Hundred Years' War (1337–1453), the Thirty Years' War (1618–1648), the First World War (1914–1918) and the Second World War (1939–1945) – were to be fought before Western Europe could achieve the current relative peace and pacification (Kingsbury, 2019; Mitchell and Fazi, 2017; Reiter and Stam, 2002). Over those hundreds of years, Western societies have gone through fundamental formations and transformations. The fundamental changes, often revolutions, have produced the current developments in those societies. It will easily be inferred, then, that several conditions are needed to be in place in order for peace to prevail. The pacification of Western societies is a production of several generations of evolution, and historical, social, political, cultural and economic transformation (Smith, 1986). Drawing lessons from the historical experience, it should not be difficult to understand that peacebuilding requires time and a lot of effort. Moreover, it is the outcome of an interplay of internal actors and structures that occur over gradual historical trajectories. In addition, as this book has emphasised, it is primarily a domestic task and responsibility.

This chapter will address the issue of peacebuilding deriving from two theoretical notions: state emancipation and societal pacification. This conceptualisation draws on the long historical and sociological tradition of societal transformation embedded in the theoretical and conceptual understanding, interpretation and analysis of the evolutionary process of nation and state formation. State emancipation and societal pacification in the process of historical societal construction: nation and state formation is understood as a simultaneous gradual process. It is conceptualised as a simultaneous genesis and trajectory that occurs not necessarily under intentional and purposive act of specific state agents, particularly in the first phase of formation (proto). Rather, it is a complementary process whose eventual outcome became state emancipation and societal pacification. Emancipation and pacification evolve simultaneously leading to state control over society, yet ultimately power rests on the people therefore checks and balance guide the state–society relationship. This dialectical relation characterises the simultaneous process of emancipation and pacification. The point of departure here is sustainable and functional peace and peacebuilding is primarily a domestic process that concerns domestic actors, structures, culture, history and situation. As such, it reflects and is dictated by internal interests and power relations. To stress again, and leaning on the literature of formation and transformation, the process is primarily propelled by the interplay between actors and structures defining society at a particular time.

The major challenge for the post-colonial state in Africa, in its formation and transformation process, has been to emancipate itself from societal group influence and pacification of society under the territory it controls. Emancipation means ensuring sovereignty. A sovereign state enjoys both internal and external legitimacy in governing the citizens and territory in its domain and in dealing with other states (Young, 1994: 28–29). Legitimacy has sociological and legal dimensions. While sociologically, it may refer to the internal, legally it refers to the external (Henderson, 2015; Jackson and Rosberg, 1984; Schaar, 2000). Internality of legitimacy accounts for state–society relationship, and is guided by the fact that society confers legitimacy on the state. Legality, on the other hand, is associated with the international legal system that defines inter-state relationship. It relies on the Westphalian Treaty where from states extract their external legal status and join the club of states. Nevertheless, the harsh reality is that the situation in post-colonial Africa, far from being mono-sovereignty (where the state has the benefit of absolute sovereignty) is characterised by the duality of sovereignty. In principle, the emancipation of the state demonstrates the emergence of a mature, developed, peaceful state – a state that is capable of building society and societal institutions, mechanisms and infrastructures that foster peace and advance peacebuilding. The reverse is also true, in that society constructs a strong state that represents it. In post-colonial Africa, state shoulders the responsibility of nation formation, because state precedes nation, giving rise to the connotation of state–nation (Smith, 1983). The connotation of state–nation with regard to Africa, and nation-state in the context of the West may be a misrepresentation, because it was the absolutist feudal state that created the nation in Europe too.

Peacebuilding in this sense may presuppose the pacification of societal groups. The structures and relationship between state emancipation and societal pacification, in modern times, are regulated by a balanced state of coexistence, where state and society – acting as complements, with checks and balances – propel this business. In the final analysis, it is society that controls the state, since power emanates from the people. This chapter examines the mechanisms through which emancipation and pacification are generated, and how they constitute a prerequisite for enduring peacebuilding. The next section addresses the issue of state emancipation. Then comes an analysis of societal pacification, followed by a section on state penetration. The last section provides some concluding remarks.

State emancipation

The dialectics governing the relationship between state emancipation and societal pacification is framed in such a way that we cannot understand the one without the other. In other words, the one is a condition of the other, but not in a sequential chronology. This section analyses state emancipation. The premise of the emancipation of the state relates to the emergence of three interrelated situations: (i) autonomy of the state, (ii) a state that stands above societal groups, (iii) the establishment of state hegemony over society (Bereketeab, 2011; Chabal and Daloz, 1999; Young, 1994). State autonomy means independence of the state to exercise legitimate authority and control over society, without interference by other societal agencies or groups. As an institution, the state should emerge as an autonomous organ vis-à-vis societal groups. Without that autonomy, the state would not be able to exercise legitimate authority, an authority that presupposes voluntary acceptance. State hegemony over society refers to the monopoly of the means of violence. This way the state commands authoritative and legitimate power over societal groups. Centrifugal forces are tamed and domesticated, so that they are not capable of threatening, through coercive means, the exercise of power by the state. Most importantly, they are not capable of mobilising and organising sections of society for the primary purpose of undermining the powers of the state. This is of crucial importance in polyethnic, polyglottic and polylingual setting. Many states in Africa, at one or another time, shared the means of violence with competing armed groups where the armed groups control a big part of the country. Al Shebab controls a large part of Somalia;

a big portion of DRC is controlled by various rebel groups; the central government in South Sudan lost control more than half of the territory when a civil war broke out in 2013. Mali, Liberia, Libya, Sierra Leone, Angola, Central African Republic, Sudan, etc. at one or another time lost control of their territory to societal groups. In such situation, the central state represents only a section of society that undermines its autonomy and consequently loses legitimacy.

The legitimate exercise of authority presupposes the standing of the state above societal groups, where it proves its neutrality in relation to, and in the equal treatment of, societal groups based on class, ethnicity, religion, gender, generation, linguistic diversity, etc. The establishment of an uncontested hegemonic state position over society arising through the instrumentality of coercive and administrative apparatuses (Ake, 2000; Callaghy, 1984; Weber, 1948) is arguably perceived as an indication of the evolution of the modern state (Christensen and Laitin, 2019: 70). The Weberian conceptualisation of the state as the sole body entitled to exercise a legitimate monopoly on violence underpins sovereignty. This monopoly on violence is intimately linked to the pacification of society, as an unpacified society competes with the state in wielding the means of violence. This contention is, however, predicated on the assumption that the state's hegemonic position should serve society, because ultimate power rests with society. But also, it is society that has voluntarily surrendered some rights to the state in exchange for security, as per the social contract theory. State legitimacy is predicated on its ability to deliver social goods. A state that fails in its cardinal function of delivery to all of its citizens equally is certainly to be challenged by all or some citizens.

In sum, then the three situations constituting emancipation characterise an evolved modern state. The evolution of a modern state, in turn, is the outcome of the pacification of society and the emancipation of the state, which heralds peace and enhances peacebuilding, given that the state is *prima facie* a peace-builder, as it is a war-maker (Richmond, 2013). An essential presumption of this argument is that centrifugal forces should submit themselves to the power of the central state. There should not be any parallel authorities with the right to exercise legitimate coercive power. Unfortunately, as the examples above illustrate, the reality defining post-colonial African state is that more than often it is challenged by centrifugal forces. Indeed, it is not rare that centrifugal forces control a big chunk of the territory and establish a parallel loci of power. This is an indication of the yet ongoing process of state formation and immaturity of the state, leading some scholars to claim the existence of de jure state but not de facto (Jackson and Rosberg, 1982).

Statebuilding presumes the emancipation of the state from society, since societal groups need to subordinate an omnipresent and omnipotent state. In other words, the purpose and process of statebuilding is to construct and bring forth a political organisation that strictly represents the people within the territory it claims to control (Brinkerhoff, 2007; Kingsbury, 2019), and at the same time it stands above societal groups, maintaining its autonomy. State emancipation engenders the submission of society to the will of the former. The state assumes its hegemonic position by subordinating centrifugal societal forces through authoritative powers, rather than by depending solely on coercive instruments. It commands moral authority, where society willingly obeys the state's orders. A state that has not gone through this transformation process is presumed to be weak, because it still shares its authority with other centrifugal forces. 'The development of a modern state depends above all on the gradual emancipation of established political structures from society' (Chabal and Daloz, 1999: 4–5). A divided authority would imply deficiency in the legitimacy of the state. According to this understanding, a properly emancipated state could easily be institutionalised (lack of proper institutionalisation being another source of state weakness and source of conflict and instability). The implication is that moral authority is conferred on institutions, not on the personalities that occupy those institutions. Moreover, the state is a set of institutions. These represent familiarity, patterns, objectivity, neutrality, professionalism, predictability, transparency, neutrality and routine – consequently trust and respect that citizens easily recognise and abide by.

Lack of institutionalisation, it is assumed, leads to the personalisation of power and politics. This in turn implies subjectivity, impulsiveness, unfamiliarity, unpredictability and system instability. Moreover, it implies the state is captured by sectarian groups or powerful individuals who do not represent the whole citizenry. The non-emancipation of the state in Africa is attributed partly to the nature of the colonial state – a state both arbitrarily and poorly bureaucratised (Chabal and Daloz, 1999: 4). Rightly, Chabal and Daloz trace the non-emancipation of the state to its colonial foundation. They contend that the non-emancipation is because the state did not sprout from the womb of society. Being an alien body, it simply floated above society and tried to impose its wishes from a distance. This imposition is reliant on the exercise of crude forces. It never succeeded in penetrating society, since it did not spring from the local society as such; therefore, the issue of its emancipation was rendered irrelevant. The entire notion of state emancipation rests on the assumption that state and society are intimately entwined. It is only a

closely bound state–society configuration that would require emancipation. Overall, a non-emancipated state could not engender peace, and
peacebuilding would encounter insurmountable hurdles. As an instrument of oppression and exploitation, the *raison d'être* of the colonial
state was to extract resources on behalf of capital back home, not to be
concerned with the institutionalisation and bureaucratisation of local
institutions and structures, which are salient prerequisites for enduring
state emancipation and peacebuilding. Finally, Chabal and Daloz (1999:
4–5) argue, 'The development of modern state depends above all on the
gradual emancipation of established political structures from society'.

The concept of dual sovereignty (Tilly, 1978) appropriately captures
the prevailing condition in many of the states of Africa. Duality of
sovereignty denotes the prevalence of parallel loci of power, competing for legitimate dominance and existing side by side, impeding the
emergence of the conditions that would lead to absolute hegemony of
a central state. Duality of sovereignty is a symptomatic characteristic
of a stage of transition in societal formation. Societies, in their transition from traditionality to modernity, display behaviour of dual sovereignty. The sociological literature suggests that the ephemeral nature
of duality – as a staging post in the transition – finds resolution when
the modern formation of state and society is completed, and when
balance and equilibrium, as a characteristic of the developed stage,
is stored.

The prevalence of mutually exclusive centrifugal forces that engender parity (symmetry) between state and society renders the statebuilding process extremely feeble. Broadly, in terms of their relationship,
state and society in Africa could be described as still fused together
both functionally and structurally: that is, there is no clear delineation
or differentiation between society and state, which is a characteristic feature of a modern state. This is due partly to the alien origin of
the colonial state (as mentioned earlier), and partly to the failure of
the post-colonial nationalist leaders to integrate the state into society,
allowing the continuation of two publics or institutional bifurcation
(Ekeh, 1975; Mamdani, 1996). The clear delineation between state and
society in the process of peacebuilding is supposed to fulfil two objectives. The first is that the state, as both war-maker and peace-maker,
is checked and counter-checked by society. The second is that society, as the ultimate power holder, carves out its own space, without
any meddling by the state (as is the case in state–society fusion). This
space is then used by society to make sure that peacebuilding is advanced through the generation of a harmonious, pacified, integrated
and amicable relationship (Paffenholz, 2015: 859). Societal checks on

the state are carried out through representative institutions that curb powers of the state. Such institutions include constitution, legislative organ, cultural and religious institutions, civil society associations and community-based organisations. The state conducts business based on the discretionary power provided to it by the societal representative institutions and mechanisms.

A critical question, however, is how emancipated and autonomous is the state from societal forces, and more importantly from the market? Is the theoretical assumption adequately corroborated by empirical evidence and reality? Citing Carl Schmitt, Lazzarato (2015: 70) writes: 'The social state, he [Schmitt] argues, no longer has any political autonomy because it is in the grip of the social and economic forces of capitalism.' Accentuating Schmitt's conception, Michel Foucault (2008) also argues that the capitalist state no longer retains its sovereignty, but rather is under the control of capital and its development. Therefore, sovereignty does not stem from the people, or from democracy, or from the nation, but from capital. This means, then, that the state capital captured by certain societal groups alienates others, which means that neutrality – and its status above any societal group – is highly compromised. This compromised status belies the emancipation of the state, since it becomes rather partisan and not a guarantor of general interest. Both the neoliberal state, with its profound entrenchment in capital and the market, and those who sit at the helm of it have forfeited the emancipation aspired to, and predicted by, progressive humanist thinkers disposed to engender an equilibrium between state and society. The appropriation of the state by capital and the market in a neoliberal world has perhaps terminally disrupted the state–society balance. The supremacy of capital and the market, where the state (and governance) is geared to facilitating their success and function, now extends beyond its (state's) spatio-temporal borders to the global south, and particularly Africa (cf. Lazzarato, 2015). Structural adjustment programmes (SAPs), military interventions and the scramble for resources on behalf of certain societal groups provide evidence of the globalising process. Moreover, these external interventions play the role of disruption in the state–society balance. The state may be integrated in the pyramidal structured globalised world, while the overwhelming rural population is left behind.

In the conventional view, the evolution of a modern state presupposes, among other things, the separation of the state and society (Chabal and Daloz, 1999; Young, 1994). The process of separation duly involves two interrelated processes: state emancipation and societal pacification occurring within a defined space and time. This clear delineation is presumed to have a contributing effect to peace and peacebuilding. In this sense, peacebuilding is not only a process but also a condition.

Societal pacification

The other related concept is pacification. Pacification is commonly understood as a situation of peacefulness, mode of life in which amicable and peaceful means and instruments become the sole manner of resolving conflicts. It is a life characterised by peace, harmony and equilibrium. The pacification of society entails two dimensions: internal and external. In the internal dimension, the most salient condition of the evolution of the state refers to the domination of the state where the submission of society is a necessary prerequisite. The variables of domination and submission, as voluntary politico-cultural and historical expressions of an evolved modern state, have to be embedded in emergent national institutions and structures, in order to ensure their sustainability. The development of such state institutions and structures, coupled with the disarming of centrifugal societal forces, produces a mature state. This state lives in peace and harmony with society. The history of ideas treats the emergence of the state as a fundamental product of the process of protracted pacification, where the State of Nature is replaced by the state of culture, pursuant to the massive material and cultural transformation.

Classical social contract theorists, such as Thomas Hobbes, Jean-Jacques Rousseau and John Locke, were greatly puzzled by the process of transformation from the State of Nature to the state of culture, pre-society or simply state. To these scholars of social contract, the State of Nature represented the absence of government and laws to regulate human beings (Laskar, 2013). For Hobbes, the State of Nature represented a dark age of human history, where 'war of all against all' predominated. To escape the chaotic State of Nature, humanity had to invent a political organisation called the 'state' (Hobbes, 1962). To gain certain common benefits, people had to surrender voluntarily some of their sovereignty. Based on the covenant, the state assumed the legitimate right to exercise violence within the territory it controlled on behalf of society (Weber, 1948). The rationality and legitimacy of the exercise of coercion over those who deviate from the general consensus derives from the initial voluntary contract and covenant. In this historical context, it is society that pacifies itself and authorises the state rather than the state arrogating to itself the means of coercion.

For Locke, on the other hand, the State of Nature represented absolute freedom of the individual – a state of liberty, albeit with some critical deficiency. For him, the State of Nature was a Golden Age (Laskar, 2013: 3). But it was pre-political. In order to remedy this deficiency, therefore, the state was invented. Yet, the state needed to protect life and property. To regulate the relationship between society and state, there had to be a social contract. Social contract theorists argue that, in order to overcome the State of Nature, humans entered two agreements: *Pactum Unionis* and *Pactum Subjectionis*. While the first sought to ensure protection of their life and property through the construction of society, the second was an agreement that enabled them to submit to an authority and surrender their freedom and rights to it (Mouritz, 2010; Ritchie, 1891). Accordingly, they agreed to form a society by collectively and reciprocally renouncing the rights they had in the State of Nature. They had to agree to live together under common laws and to create an enforcement mechanism for the social contract and the laws that constituted it. Once they agree on basic common law, they surrender to it and the body that is chosen to enforce it. For Rousseau, the State of Nature was happiness and equality. The invention of property, however, heralded humanity's fall from grace. To correct the fall, humans needed to surrender their right to the 'general will' embedded in the social contract. In short, 'the authority or the government or the sovereign or the state came into being because of the two agreements' (Laskar, 2013: 1). This concerns the legitimacy of power. Power is construed as being legitimate on the basis of its origin and the manner in which it is exercised (Wiafe-Amoako, 2016: 78; Zaum, 2012: 51). In this context, it is driven by certain values, norms, belief systems, shared goals and expectations, institutions and mechanisms where broad consensus reigns. These in turn are constructed in a protracted historical process and societal interaction. Sources of legitimacy are presumed to be both domestic and external (Coggins, 2014; Jackson and Rosberg, 1984; Osiander, 2001). In an ideal situation, state legitimacy conflates the domestic and external dimensions equally. Most of the time, however, one dominates the other.

The external dimension of pacification relates to ensuring territorial integrity, sovereignty, security and good international relations reminiscent of the Westphalian state (Coggins, 2014: 8; Evans and Newnham, 1990; Morgenthau, 1985; Osiander, 2001: 261). The Westphalian Treaty was perceived to generate societal pacification. This is translated to mean contributing to and living in a neighbourhood where amicable peace prevails. The amicability is also a function of a broader internalisation of pacification that governs inter-state relations. This produces procedures and norms that render inter-state relations predictability, stability, normalcy and rule-driven game. The contemporary post-Cold War – which some term post-Westphalian (Kreuder-Sonnen and Zangl, 2014; Newman et al., 2009: 6–7) – neoliberal ideology-driven campaign has disrupted the status quo in international relations, leading to serious conflicts and instabilities all over the world. The neoliberal ideological strategy to mobilise non-state actors, which involves armed opposition, to counter-balance the state is a clear measure of undermining societal pacification. Forgetting their history of societal pacification, Western powers engage in abetting and support centrifugal forces in the aim of regime change. This act is countering the work and process of pacification in developing societies, and particularly in Africa, with dire consequences. Supporting and arming anti-Saddam forces in Iraq, anti-Gaddafi forces in Libya and anti-Assad forces in Syria (Held and Ulrichsen, 2011), or arming warlords of anti-Union of Islamic Courts in Somalia (Muller, 2013; Samatar, 2013) are good illustrations of the post-Cold War and post-Westphalian interventionist policy that undermines the pacification of society. These acts contribute to the emergence of centrifugal forces competing for the means of coercion and domination. The push to limit the state, and in turn replace its roles with CS, NGOs and other non-state actors, is an indication of the hostile position of neoliberal ideology towards African states (Tom, 2017: 32–34). What is needed is strengthening the state and state institutions, and democratisation of the state. A weak state cannot be democratised. The emergence of private paramilitary and security forces that overtake state functions are signs of non-pacification of society. For instance, the appropriation of central state functions by paramilitaries in Colombia demonstrates the failure of the state to control its territory, but also lack of pacification of society (Acemoglu and Robinson, 2013. 377–382). Western states are widely using private security companies in Africa. These private securities are not only undermining the state because they take functions of the state, but also are accountable to no one that allow them to get away with any crime (Dias, 2013; Higate and Utas, 2017).

The post-Cold War and post-Westphalian push of non-state actors (with the aim of challenging the state) and the drive for regime change (for the purposes of democratisation) by contrast encourage centrifugal forces. Instead of pacification, this may lead to militantism in society, thereby countering the peace, peacebuilding and pacification process in a developing society. The upshot of this, particularly in Africa, is the disruption of the gradual pacification process, with dire consequences for peace and peacebuilding. A pacified society is presumed to be one that has surrendered the means of violence to the state. Otherwise, 'The state may be viewed as a ruling organization that competes for power with other political, economic, and social organizations and groups' (Callaghy, 1984: 90). The competition between state and society eventually has to be resolved in favour of the state with regard to the means of coercion, in order for centrifugal forces to be pacified and tamed. The state as an institution is an abstract concept that is empirically concretised in its expression through its component entities – executive, legislature, judiciary and bureaucracy – that receive societal legitimacy. This development enhances peace and peacebuilding engendered by pacification. Of course, the state itself is expected to abide by the social contract that it enters into implicitly with its citizens, and to submit itself to the general popular will – a general will whose genealogy of sovereignty and legitimacy springs from the people in mutually reinforcing social contract (Bereketeab, 2008). In other words the fountain of ultimate power is the people.

State penetration

The theoretical assumption of state emancipation and societal pacification as necessary requirements for sustainable peacebuilding rests on another theoretical premise of state penetration. The notion of state and society as an analytical binary is predicated on the dialectics of simultaneous fusion and rupture. Fusion represents the presupposition of the two in unison – as with Siamese twins – while rupture represents the autonomous existence and functioning of the respective entities. From this it follows that there is an existential necessity for the state to penetrate society. On the other hand, also, society ultimately retains the power to restrain the state. When the state penetrates society either marginally or not at all, state–society relations are characterised by abnormality and dysfunctionality. This is so because the two entities stand aloof when it becomes difficult to exert mutual influence. Peace and peacebuilding are arguably contingent on the symmetrical fusion of state and society. This fusion inexorably constitutes a prerequisite for state penetration. State penetration of society is achieved through the presence of state institutions at every level of society – village, district, province and national. Physical presence alone is not enough. Those state institutions should be able to deliver services at every level of the ladder as fulfilment of their social contract obligation. Social contract is tied to citizenship, while citizenship is expressed in duties and rights.

State penetration varies in degrees in different historical periods and types of state. It is important to note that emancipation, pacification and penetration are phenomena of modernity. Their development is a consequence of – and is guided by – the emergence of a modern mode of organisation. The absolutist feudal state never succeeded in penetrating society. The king ruled through lords, nobles and vassals who curved their own fiefdoms. This kind of political system was less amenable to state penetration of society. The state lacked capacity and technology, even the intention. This means that penetration is governed by whatever nature, capacity and material infrastructure that the state possesses at a particular point in its developmental trajectory. It is also contingent on the relations, diversity and interplay of social forces, and on the nature of the historical process of formation of the state. Ultimately, it depends on intentions of providing indemnities to citizens.

Today, state penetration is extremely high in Western societies. The great advancement of technology enables the state to penetrate and control society. Using social security number and through smart phones, the state in the West exerts unprecedented penetration and control, not only on its own citizens but also globally. The technology of penetration and control in the service of the state in the West makes Western societies the most penetrated and controlled. This led to some scholars talk about surveillance society (Lyon, 2001).

With regard to Africa, it could be possible to distinguish at least three historical periods and concomitant types of state: pre-colonial, colonial and post-colonial. It is a historical fact that state penetration in the different periods and types show a degree and magnitude of variation that have implications for peace and peacebuilding. The pre-colonial period in the African history of state formation is markedly different from the subsequent colonial and post-colonial ones. The chief feature of the pre-colonial African state was the decentralised and parcelised nature of the territorial polity (Ake, 2000; Mamdani, 2017). In a situation where kings and chiefs, primarily concentrating in ruling their own community or ethnic group, and where governing, in terms of territoriality, was highly amorphous and diffuse, the question of state penetration of society had no meaning. Beyond territoriality as a basis of organisation and identity formation, the penetration and cohesion of society based on ethnicity/community identity formation were much more concrete and intimate in the pre-colonial period. The colonial state's territorial delineation and delimitation, political and administrative centralisation and hierarchisation necessitated penetration. This is so because territorialisation brought together different entities in terms of both territoriality and demography (ethnicity), which required a different form of penetration. Yet, as the state was an alien authority, its scope for penetration was highly limited. Colonial authorities chose to govern local communities through selected local messengers, in the British system, known as indirect rule (Mamdani, 2017). This messengerial rule precluded state penetration at the community level. Those post-colonial states that emerged from a protracted liberation struggle may have had a better chance of penetrating society. This is because – unlike those that assumed power through the peaceful transfer from a colonial authority – national liberation states began their ascendency to state power from remote corners of the country. This gave them the opportunity to explore and penetrate society (see Bereketeab, 2018). In other words, while those leaders of post-colonial state who were handed over power from colonial authorities remained urban-centred, leaders of national liberation states rose to power from remote villages that allowed them to penetrate their societies. The ascendency to state power through societal stairs that stretch along village, district, province and nation has a better possibility of state penetration.

One of the contributions of colonialism to statebuilding is territorial and political centralisation. This centralisation assumed two dimensions in the exercise of power: direct rule and indirect rule, which spawned decentralisation within the overarching centralisation. This phenomenon is described as 'decentralised despotism' (Mamdani, 2017) and 'two publics' (Ekeh, 1975). Ekeh's 'two publics' is a treatise on the evolution of the segregation into the urban sphere and the rural sphere. The emergence of two antagonistic social spaces within the supposedly territorially and politically centralised state illustrates the contradictions and anomalies of colonialism. Socio-economic centralisation and integration that followed colonial territorial integration was not accompanied by national cultural integration.

The emergence of two distinct public spheres under colonialism generated a dual system of rule that precluded state penetration. This state of affair continued into post-colonial times, when the post-colonial state – in spite of its claim to represent both publics – remained poorly penetrative, because the two publics created by colonialism continued as parallel systems, negatively impacting on emancipation, pacification and penetration as prerequisites for peacebuilding and statebuilding (PBSB). This condition rendered the post-colonial state in Africa conflict-prone, unstable, devastated by civil wars and other forms of conflicts and crises. This, in turn, induced the neoliberal world order to prescribe neoliberal PBSB to reconfigure conflict societies in a Western mould, which further exposed the societies to more fragility and crisis.

State penetration of society in post-colonial Africa – as a prerequisite for peace and peacebuilding in a territorially defined identity – as in the colonial, and in contrast to a pre-colonial ethnically defined identity, required a different form. It also required different levels. The multi-ethnic nature of the post-colonial territorial nation was very much dependent on the socialisation of citizens of the state into civic territorial identity. The success of the post-colonial socialisation, internalisation and externalisation project determined the level of state penetration, societal pacification and peacebuilding in Africa. The success also signifies an achievement in societal construction.

Conclusion

This chapter has examined state emancipation and societal pacification as prerequisites for peacebuilding. It has argued that the pacification of society – allowing the means of coercion to be the sole prerogative of the state and precluding non-state groups from possessing or exercising the means of coercion – is a fundamental necessity for the pacification of society, which in turn is necessary for peace and peacebuilding. The other face of the coin is state emancipation. State emancipation refers to autonomy of the state. This autonomy concerns the state's position against centrifugal social forces. Both rest on the assumption that there is an intimate and dialectical intertwining of state and society. But, often, external intervention disrupts the evolution of an amicable and balanced relationship. This intervention and disruption has grown in scope and momentum in the wake of the Cold War.

In this state–society relationship, the state gains the autonomy it deserves – an autonomy that enables it to exercise power over class, ethnic, religious and regional societal groups. This autonomy is also contingent on the supremacy of the state over societal centrifugal groups. According to this conception, state emancipation and societal pacification gradually consolidate the autonomy of the state. Societal pacification also emancipates the state in order to fulfil its external functional tasks of defending the integrity and security of society from external forces. A lack of state emancipation means that sectarian social groups dominate power, which gives rise to a real or imagined sense of marginalisation among groups. This sense of marginalisation further leads to ethnic and clan strife, resulting in chronic civil wars. Underpinning this situation is the state's failure to represent equally the entire spectrum of social cleavages. On the other hand, lack of emancipation and pacification also implies an absence of the consensual and contractual relationship between state and society that is a prerequisite for peace and peacebuilding.

Furthermore, the perception of emancipation and pacification is predicated on another perception: the perception of penetration. In order for emancipation and pacification to serve as an analytical and empirical tool for understanding peacebuilding, they need to be embedded in the state penetration of society. Under circumstances where the state fails to adequately penetrate society, emancipation and pacification are devoid of meaning, which would indicate that peacebuilding becomes a remote possibility. In a more substantial sense, the sustainability of societal pacification and state emancipation rests on the institutionalisation and democratisation of the state. Above all, it depends on a simultaneous separation of state and society, on the one hand, and on their cohesion, on the other.

The historical genesis and trajectory of the evolution of state emancipation and societal pacification is understood to be a product of a gradual and piecemeal evolution leading to modernity and the emergence of modern societies. Modernity and modernisation in this sense is not to be conceptualised as Westernisation and Westernity. In addition, it is perceived to be the product of a transformational process from a state of war to a state of culture. The theoretical and philosophical assumption undergirding the transformation process is the gradual evolutionary development leading to societal construction: nation and state formation. According to this assumption, state emancipation and societal pacification are a simultaneous process embodied in the transformation. Presumably, Western societies went through this transformation process, hence the prevalence of peace and stability. The reason African societies and developing societies in general are still embroiled in chronic conflicts and wars could be that they have not yet passed through the evolutionary transformation process. Of course, this unilinear evolutionary conception of the history of state and society development is fraught with a number of theoretical, conceptual and methodological problems, which I cannot discuss here. Nevertheless, one thing is clear: state and nation formation is a historical process that requires enough time to elapse, but it is also a domestic process that should be fashioned according to the popular progressive model.

References

Acemoglu, Daron and Robinson, James A. 2013. *Why Nations Fail: The Origin of Power, Prosperity and Poverty*. London: Profile Books LTD.

Ake, Claude. 2000. *The Feasibility of Democracy in Africa*. Dakar: Council for the Development of Social Science Research in Africa (CODESRIA).

Bereketeab, Redie (ed.). 2018. *National Liberation Movements as Government in Africa*. London and New York: Routledge.

Bereketeab, Redie. 2011. 'Rethinking State Building in the Horn of Africa: Challenges of Striking a Balance between Traditional and Modern Institutions', *African Studies*, vol. 70, no. 3, pp. 376–392.

Bereketeab, Redie. 2008. 'State Building Project of Peace-Building in the Horn of Africa', in Ulf Johansson (ed.), *Post-Conflict Peacebuilding in the Horn of Africa*. Lund: Lund University, pp. 37–53.

Brinkerhoff, Derick W. (ed.). 2007. *Governance in Post-Conflict Societies: Rebuilding Fragile States*. London and New York: Routledge.

Callaghy, Thomas M. 1984. *The State–Society Struggle: Zaire in Comparative Perspective*. New York: Columbia University Press.

Chabal, Patrick and Daloz, Jean-Pascal. 1999. *Africa Works: Disorder as Political Instrument*. Oxford, Bloomington and Indianapolis, IN: James Currey and Indiana University Press.

Christensen, Darin and Laitin, David D. 2019. *African States since Independence: Order, Development, and Democracy*. New Haven, CT and London: Yale University Press.

Coggins, Bridget. 2014. *Power Politics and State Formation in the Twentieth Century: The Dynamics of Recognition*. New York: Cambridge University Press.

Dias, Alexandra Magnolia (ed.). 2013. *State and Societal Challenges in the Horn of Africa: Conflict and Processes of State Formation, Reconfiguration and Disintegration*. Lisboa: Centro de Estudos Internacionais.

Ekeh, Peter P. 1975. 'Colonialism and the Two Publics in Africa: A Theoretical Statement', *Comparative Studies in Society and History*, vol. 17, no. 1, pp. 91–112.

Evans, Graham and Newnham, Jeffrey. 1990. *The Dictionary of World Politics: A Reference Guide to Concepts, Ideas, and Institutions*. Hemel Hempstead: Harvester Wheatsheaf.

Foucault, Michel. 2008. *The Birth of Biopolitics*. London: Palgrave Macmillan.

Held, David and Ulrichsen, Kristian Coates. 2011. 'War of Decline: Afghanistan, Iraq and Libya', *Open Democracy*, 12 December.

Henderson, Errol A. 2015. *African Realism? International Relations Theory and Africa's Wars in the Postcolonial Era*. Lanham, MD and London: Rowman and Littlefield.

Higate, Paul and Utas, Mats (eds.). 2017. *Private Security in Africa: From the Global Assemblage to the Everyday*. London: Zed Books.

Hobbes, Thomas. 1962 [1651]. *Leviathan*. New York: Macmillan.

Jackson, Robert and Rosberg, Carl G. 1984. 'Popular Legitimacy in African Multi-Ethnic States', *Journal of Modern African Studies*, vol. 22, no. 2, pp. 177–198.

Jackson, Robert and Rosberg, Carl. 1982. 'Why Africa's Weak States Persist: The Empirical and Juridical in Statehood', *World Politics*, vol. 35, no. 1, pp. 1–24.

Kingsbury, Damien. 2019. *Politics in Developing Countries*. London and New York: Routledge.

Kreuder-Sonnen, Christian and Zangl, Bernhard. 2014. 'Which Post-Westphalia? International Organizations between Constitutionalism and Authoritarianism', *European Journal of International Relations*, vol. 2, no. 3, pp. 568–594.

96 State emancipation and societal pacification

96 *State emancipation and societal pacification*

96   *State emancipation and societal pacification*

96   *State emancipation and societal pacification*

96   *State emancipation and societal pacification*

Laskar, Manzoor Elahi. 2013. 'Summary of Social Contract Theory by Hobbes, Locke and Rousseau', Symbiosis Law School, Pune.

Lazzarato, Mauricio. 2015. 'Neoliberalism, the Financial Crisis and the End of the Liberal State', *Theory, Culture and Society*, vol. 37, no. 7–8, pp. 67–83.

Lyon, David. 2001. *Surveillance Society: Monitoring Everyday Life*. Maidenhead: McGraw-Hill Education.

Mamdani, Mahmood. 2017. *Citizen and Subject: Contemporary Africa and the Legacy of Late Colonialism, with a New Preface*. Johannesburg and Kampala: Wits University Press and Makerere Institute of Social Research.

Mamdani, Mahmood. 1996. *Citizens and Subjects: Contemporary Africa and the Legacy of Late Colonialism*. Princeton, NJ: Princeton University Press.

Mitchell, William and Fazi, Thomas. 2017. *Reclaiming the State: A Progressive Vision of Sovereignty for a Post-Neoliberal World*. London: Pluto Press.

Morgenthau, Hans J. 1985. *Politics among Nations: The Struggle for Power and Peace*, 6th ed. Revised and edited by Kenneth W. Thompson. New York: McGraw-Hill.

Mouritz, Thomas. 2010. 'Comparing the Social Contracts of Hobbes and Locke', *The Western Australian Jurist*, vol. 1, pp. 123–127.

Muller, Bjorn. 2013. 'Militia and Piracy in the Horn of Africa: External Response', in Redie Bereketeab (ed.), *The Horn of Africa: Intra-State and Inter-State Conflicts and Security*. London: Pluto Press, pp. 178–196.

Newman, Edward, Paris, Roland and Richmond, Oliver P. 2009. 'Introduction', in Edward Newman, Roland Paris and Oliver P. Richmond (eds.), *New Perspectives on Liberal Peace-Building*. Tokyo and New York: United Nations University Press, pp. 3–25.

Osiander, Andreas. 2001. 'Sovereignty, International Relations, and the Westphalian Myth', *International Organization*, vol. 55, no. 2, pp. 251–287.

Paffenholz, Thania. 2015. 'Unpacking the Local Turn in Peace-Building: A Critical Assessment towards an Agenda for Future Research', *Third World Quarterly*, vol. 36, no. 5, pp. 857–874.

Reiter, Dan and Stam, Allan C. 2002. *Democracies at War*. Princeton, NJ and Oxford: Princeton University Press.

Richmond, Oliver P. 2013. 'The Legacy of State Formation Theory for Peacebuilding and Statebuilding', *International Peacekeeping*, vol. 20, no. 3, pp. 299–315.

Ritchie, David G. 1891. 'Contribution to the History of the Social Contract Theory', *Political Science Quarterly*, vol. 6, no. 4, pp. 656–676.

Samatar, Abdi Ismail. 2013. 'The Production of Somali Conflict and the Role of Internal and External Actors', in Redie Bereketeab (ed.), *The Horn of Africa: Intra-State and Inter-State Conflict and Security*. London: Pluto Press, pp. 156–177.

Schaar, John H. 2000. *Legitimacy in the Modern State*. New Brunswick, NJ and Oxford: Transaction Publishers.

Smith, Anthony D. 1986. *The Ethnic Origins of Nations*. Oxford and Cambridge, MA: Blackwell.

Smith, Anthony D. 1983. *State and Nation in the Third World.* Great Britain: Wheatsheaf Books.

Tilly, Charles. 1978. *From Mobilization to Revolution.* Reading, MA: Addison Wesley.

Tom, Patrick. 2017. *Liberal Peace and Post-Conflict Peace-Building in Africa.* London: Palgrave Macmillan.

Weber, Max. 1948. *From Max Weber: Essays in Sociology.* Translated, edited and with an introduction by H. H. Gerth and C. Wright Mills. London and Boston, MA: Routledge and Kegan.

Wiafe-Amoako, Francis. 2016. 'Legitimacy and Rule: Africa in Search of a Political Order', in Ali A. Mazrui and Francis Wiafe-Amoako (eds.), *African Institutions: Challenges to Political, Social, and Economic Foundations of Africa's Development.* Lanham, MD and London: Rowman and Littlefield, pp. 75–95.

Young, Crawford. 1994. *The African Colonial State in Comparative Perspective.* New York and London: Yale University Press.

Zaum, Dominik. 2012. 'Statebuilding and Governance: The Conundrum of Legitimacy and Local Ownership', in Devon Curtis and Gwinyayi Dzinesa (eds.), *Peace-Building, Power, and Politics in Africa.* Athens: Ohio University Press, pp. 47–62.

5 Statebuilding and peacebuilding

Harmony and discordance

Introduction

The common understanding among donors, think tanks, IFIs and analysts is that there is harmony between statebuilding and peacebuilding (Zaum, 2012: 47). Indeed, the perception is that they complement each other (Grävingholt et al., 2009). The one is a presupposition for the other. This is clearly stated by the International Dialogue on Peacebuilding and Statebuilding when it is written as:

> The report is based on an understanding of peacebuilding and statebuilding as two mutually reinforcing processes aimed at supporting the building of effective, legitimate, accountable and responsive states characterised by a healthy state-society relationship and by peaceful relations among communities and with external neighbours.
>
> (OECD, 2010: 17)

That connection is, however, thrown into question by research and researchers, on the basis of serious empirical scientific studies. These are two different complex dimensions of societal construction. It is argued otherwise that the relationship is, in fact, characterised by contradictions and complexities. A book edited by Charles T. Call and Vanessa Wyeth (2008) is entitled *Building States to Build Peace*. Although on the face of it, the title may seem confusing, giving the impression that statebuilding is a precondition for peacebuilding, the book attempts to highlight the distinction (or discordance) between statebuilding and peacebuilding. The central argument that the authors try to convey is as follows:

> Yet the most salient finding is that the relationship between peacebuilding and state building is complicated, contingent, and

context-dependent. That is not to say that the specifics of each case prevent generalizations from being drawn. However, peace-building cannot be boiled down to building state institutions. Enhancing state institutional capacity may potentially harm the chances for consolidating peace and vice versa. A number of tensions exist between logic of building states and that of ensuring that war will not recur.

(Call and Wyeth, 2008: 3)

This quote, as well as the book in general, testifies to the fact that statebuilding is not necessarily an essential prerequisite for sustainable peacebuilding; on the contrary, there are tensions and contradictions between them. Indeed, the book demonstrates that peacebuilding and state-building are two phenomena dictated by different logic. While the logic of statebuilding is laying down institutional arrangements, the logic of peacebuilding is forestalling recurrences of war. This chapter's aim is to explore and analyse the discord and harmony that exist between peacebuilding and statebuilding (PBSB). It seeks to analyse theoretical and operational convergence and divergence in PBSB.

Indisputably, it was the perception of complementarity thought to exist between PBSB that lay behind the neoliberal peacebuilding that underpins international intervention in statebuilding (Tom, 2017). Peacebuilding, in the neoliberal approach, often follows peace deals between the warring parties and aims at institutionalisation and consolidation of the deal (Heathershaw, 2013; Paris, 2002). It is a post-conflict state-construction endeavour. As a post-conflict dispensation, it necessarily confines itself to the actors who were engaged in combat. It could therefore rightly be described as a combatants' arrangement. But the fact of the matter is often that peacebuilding involves more than the combatants, which makes it complex and time-consuming. From procedural and processual points of departure, peacebuilding is the summation of several stages that include peace-making, peace mediation and peacekeeping. Peace-making concerns willingness and readiness of combatants to strike a peace deal, mental preparation. Peace mediation and peacekeeping are borne by external actors. While peace mediation refers to the work of observers to convince the combatants to cease fighting, peacekeeping concerns the separation of combatants and stand between them to uphold the peace mediated. Peacebuilding is thus an accumulation of all these processes and procedures that make it much profound and protracted.

Neoliberal peacebuilding's concern with institutionalisation and the consolidation of a peace deal signed by warring factions alienates and marginalises certain sections of society that are affected by the conflict as much as (if not more than) the combatants. The side-lining of many sections of society from the peace process and deal is what makes it incomplete and doomed to failure. The incompleteness of the peacebuilding process would certainly lead to a reversion to conflict and war. Conflict is not simply a security issue that concerns only the combatants; it is rather a political issue, and as such requires a political solution. Resolving a conflict that is basically political in nature requires all affected stakeholders to be brought on board.

Drawing on the neoliberal perception of the harmony between statebuilding and peacebuilding, in recent years its proponents have demonstrated extreme interventionist tendencies to midwife statebuilding and peacebuilding in conflict-affected societies. This conviction is predicated on the assumption that statebuilding and peacebuilding are necessary conditions for democratic peace (Tom, 2017: 59–60). The democratic peace thesis is out there to reconfigure Africa (Call, 2008b; Curtis, 2012) in the neoliberal mould. By extension, the democratic peace thesis serves the globalisation scheme that ensures Western domination through inclusive but unequal global integration (Harrison, 2010).

The contention of this chapter is that there is actually discordance between statebuilding and peacebuilding, at least initially. This contention is supported by scholars such as Call (2008a: 3), Curtis (2012) and Robert (2012), and stems from the different premises that govern statebuilding and peacebuilding. In its theoretical orientation, the contention is also informed by the popular progressive model. Statebuilding by its very nature is political, and politics deals with power: how power is allocated; who takes what, how and when (Harrison, 2012: 167; Hyden, 2013; Schaar, 2000: 206). Moreover, politics generates winners and losers. Losers then seek alternative mechanisms to address their grievances, which leads to conflict and sometimes to war (Zaum, 2012: 48). Moreover, statebuilding is profoundly a long-term, gradual and meticulous process of societal transformation and construction that presupposes negotiations, dialogue, compromise, bargains, etc. among societal stakeholders. This is the conceptualisation of the popular progressive model. Neoliberal peacebuilding, on the other hand, is technical and administrative. It rarely addresses the root causes of conflicts, and nor does it include non-combatant stakeholders. It is also very dependent on external experts, at the expense of internal knowledge and expertise. Therefore, it can only bring temporary respite. In this context, then, statebuilding and peacebuilding display disharmony. In this manner, statebuilding and peacebuilding go their separate ways.

This chapter endeavours to flesh out the adverse relationship between peacebuilding and statebuilding. The following section examines the harmony between peacebuilding and statebuilding. The next one discusses the discordance between peacebuilding and statebuilding. The final section provides some concluding remarks.

Harmony between peacebuilding and statebuilding

As mentioned earlier, some of the general literature suggests that there is harmony between peacebuilding and statebuilding. This harmony is supposed to derive from the logic that the one is a condition for the existence of the other. Since the one cannot exist without the other, there must be harmony, seems to be the logic. Yet, empirical evidence could not corroborate the harmony logic. We should also note that the two models – neoliberal and popular progressive – have different approaches towards harmony. Let us examine the veracity of the proposed harmonious relationship. What conditions should prevail for there to be harmony in the relationship? This is a central question that might guide us in our assessment of the purported harmony (or lack thereof). The argument this section tries to advance is that harmony between peacebuilding and statebuilding can only be achieved in the popular progressive model. The rationality underpinning this argument is popular progressive concern with some of the profound features of PBSB such as root causes of conflicts, the political and domestic foundation of PBSB, societal construction (state and nation formation), indigenous mechanisms, institutions, knowledge, skills and authorities. Its methodological strategies of reaching harmony are dialogue, bargains, negotiations, conciliations, compromises, among all national stakeholders that make it inclusive, representative and participatory.

Statebuilding perceived as institution-building is a long-term process that may take several generations (Kamrava, 2000; Mamdani, 1996; Mazrui and Wiafe-Amoako, 2016; Poggi, 1978). Institution-building and institutionalisation also need to be transformed into a political culture if the process is to be recognised, accepted and appreciated by citizens. Political culture itself grows out of pragmatic, systematic and empirical practices and the ethos of socio-political real life. This political culture is generated by an exercise in real life that eventually constitutes part of the intuitive, automatic codes, symbols and praxis in space and time of society. The gestation of institutions as routinised entrenched political practices requires a considerable period of time to elapse. Political institutions, as political culture, are established as a result of protracted struggles that include negotiations, bargains, compromise, etc. Ultimately, these are reflectively and discursively expressed in transparency, predictability, openness in the exercise of political power. Moreover, accountability of the rule of the game, clear role expectations, recognised and hopefully accepted citizens' behaviour are other expressions of political institution. In short, political institutions are constructed and produced along historical trajectories that are embedded in the success, failure, happiness, sadness, mistakes, turmoil, calm, tribulations, vices and virtues of human experience. This is what makes them idiosyncratic and culture specific, gradual and processual in their development. This is the conceptualisation that the popular progressive model advances. The neoliberal cut-and-paste strategy of institution construction and production in the interventionist statebuilding approach is often followed by a failure, because replication and borrowing rarely works in the construction and evolution of political culture. It lacks depth, genuineness, authenticity and reciprocity.

Statebuilding is also, by its very nature, domestic, as stated earlier. As such, statebuilding is contingent on continuous negotiations, interpretations, bargains, trade-offs, compromises, dealings and expectations involving multiple stakeholders; this often aims at creating social consensus and equilibrium. These stakeholders, in poly-ethnic, poly-glottic and poly-religious societies are numerous. This multiplicity in turn presupposes complex and intriguing arrangements and treatments. In this context, statebuilding is concerned with societal construction, legitimacy and ownership by citizens (Tom, 2017; Zaum, 2012) – things that can be achieved through the popular progressive model. An externality that disturbs the intended social equilibrium ends up creating conflict and tension.

So-called state fragility, weakness and collapse – which supposedly make societies amenable to radicalism, fundamentalism and terrorism, which in turn subject the world to security risks – 'reinforced the association between statebuilding and peacebuilding' (Zaum, 2012: 47). This association is made on the grounds of short-term phenomena, but also fails to make the cause–effect connection, quite often intervention is the cause of these phenomena. The statebuilding and peacebuilding intervention driven by the neoliberal ideology aims at ameliorating the risk involved in state fragility, but fails to engender fundamental solutions. This premise is predicated on the imperatives of curtailing the negative implication of state fragility for the West. This concerns the fear of the consequences of the pathologies spilling over to the West and is the primary objective of interventionism. The facts on the ground, however, do not corroborate the assumed amelioration in the fragile societies themselves, particularly when it comes to the construction of functioning and sustainable states. This fact could be illustrated by years of interventions and subsequent developments in countries such as Somalia, DRC, Central African Republic, Burkina Faso, Mali and South Sudan. The reason for this is the very fact that the needs, realities, context, histories and experiences of the societies in question are not placed centre-stage. If recent developments are anything to go by, neoliberal intervention has rather thrown the world into an extremely precarious situation: cases in point are Libya, Iraq, Syria and Yemen. Neoliberal statebuilding seeks to build Western-style states in non-Western, post-conflict societies, in which 'strong institutions' define strong states that are able to ensure internal security and stability, in ways that also eliminate threats to global security and prosperity (Barnett, 2006).

Under these circumstances, the supposed harmony between statebuilding and peacebuilding becomes an illusion. Statebuilding (institution-building) is a long-term strategy; peacebuilding (consolidating peace agreements) is a short-term strategy (at least as perceived by neoliberalism). As such they are antagonistic. The ephemerality of neoliberal peacebuilding and the long-termism of statebuilding certainly represent two different tasks in time and objective. And the tasks certainly demand correspondingly different approaches, dynamics, mechanisms and methodologies.

The popular progressive approach of treating both statebuilding and peacebuilding as long-term processes might not bring quick fix but in the long run is clearly superior because it offers a functional and sustainable solution. We could then argue that it is only under the popular progressive model that harmony between PBSB could be achieved. The reason underpinning our argument is the predisposition of the popular progressive approach of gradual, evolutionary and transformative to societal construction: nation and state formation. In addition, the model also acknowledges the political and domestic nature of SBPB.

Discordance between peacebuilding and statebuilding

It should be noted from the very outset that the discordance refers to the narrow conceptualisation of PBSB advocated by donors, INGOs, the World Bank, the UN and neoliberal academia (Barnett, 2006: 88). In this context, neoliberal peacebuilding is, relatively speaking, of short duration. As discussed above, neoliberal peacebuilding is concerned chiefly with the technical and administrative-managerial nature of conflicts such as DDR, security sector reform, transforming security institutions, armed forces, police and intelligence apparatuses, the judiciary, etc. (Call, 2008b; Mac Ginty, 2008; Robert, 2012). Moreover, most of the time, the concern is with focusing on reconciling solely the belligerents. It thus endeavours to consolidate peace deals signed between belligerents. It ignores several salient issues such as power relation and allocation, socio-economic distribution and development spread, livelihood cleavages (farming-pastoralism), rural-urban cleavage, interethnic relation, identity and citizenship.

Statebuilding, on the other hand, is a long-term project and process. As such, it is geared towards institution-building. Building state institutions means not only putting in place key institutions that replace personalities, but making them acceptable to those who are affected by them: they should feel that the institutions are part of their daily lives, and guide, regulate and facilitate their lives. Citizens should develop a sense of ownership and be ready to defend the institutions. This engagement with and passion for state institutions on the part of citizens is achieved when institutions become part of the culture; when they are heeded and when they assume significant societal symbolic value. Moreover, statebuilding concerns profound foundation of societal construction, which by its very nature is domestic and protracted.

A number of features thus distinguish statebuilding and peacebuilding, impelling discordance. Referring to the discord, Graham Harrison (2012: 167) notes, 'Whereas building states is concrete, building peace is abstract; peacebuilding does not signify a specific agency to build'. In its abstract sense, peacebuilding could be understood as a state of mind, in which external agency would not be able to fix for others; rather, the citizens themselves have to go through a mental transformation that is processual, gradual, historical and transcendental. Hence the notion of societal pacification, which (as discussed earlier) is the outcome of a long and gradual transformation process. The fulfilment of the transformation renders societal pacification a mode of life.

Statebuilding, on the other hand, is agency contingent and driven. Historical agents are usually at the forefront of the project of statebuilding. With regard to the peacebuilding–statebuilding nexus, Oliver P. Richmond (2013: 299) also argues:

> Peacebuilding offers a cosmopolitan and normative vision of rights, development, and representation across societies, whereas statebuilding is the vehicle through which the neoliberal institutional and political framework in a particular version of this vision can be assumed within a specific territory.

Above all, statebuilding as a political act creates winners and losers. Normally, losers seek venues or means to address their grievances, leading to conflicts and wars, rather than peace. In this context, the relationship between statebuilding and peacebuilding, at least initially, is characterised by discordance. Discordance as benchmark of relationship, in time and space, represents level of development in the formation and transformation process. Developing societies, depending on their level of development, display differentiality or discordance in the process and structure of statebuilding and peacebuilding. This is further complicated by geographical and demographic complexities, such as highland–lowland, culture, or religious and ethnic diversity (Christensen and Laitin, 2019).

In the long term, undoubtedly, statebuilding is a prerequisite for peacebuilding. As alluded to in the preceding section, the kind of peacebuilding that is in harmony with statebuilding is the one that is based on the popular progressive, rather than the neoliberal model. The reason the popular progressive model engenders harmony between statebuilding and peacebuilding is that it is long term, gradual, piecemeal and processual. In this long-term project, statebuilding takes the time and energy needed for the gestation and construction of functional and sustainable state institutions. In terms of sequentiality, the foundations of a mature state need to be laid down first, in order to ensure functional and lasting peace and peacebuilding. Moreover, SBPB has to be domestic – designed, implemented and owned by nationals, without undue interference from external actors.

Statebuilding as a political project is concerned with power, and it generates winners and losers, which can lead to conflict and war. At least initially, then, it is at loggerheads with peacebuilding, which strives to bring together all stakeholders, with the aim of reconciling them. In the long run, however, statebuilding is a necessary requirement for peace and peacebuilding. The state is an agent of war and peace; hence a mature state will create the conditions necessary for peace. Eventually, there will come a time when it is imperative to have harmony between statebuilding and peacebuilding. Until that time comes, a discursive analytical segregation of the two processes is not only possible, but also an imperative requirement and function.

Conclusion

The literature on PBSB is fraught with contradictions and ambiguities. These are particularly in evidence when it comes to the relationship between statebuilding and peacebuilding. Part of the literature proposes the existence of harmony between the two; that body of literature advocates neoliberal PBSB. The popularity of neoliberal PBSB picked up momentum in the aftermath of the Cold War. The new world order that emerged then provided Western powers, led by the USA, with a free hand to shape and reconfigure non-Western conflict-ridden societies. Therefore, pervasive interventionist policies were pursued by the Western powers to mend post-war societies. It was believed that building states on the Western model, by administering a large dose of neoliberal medicine, would stabilise weak and fragile societies. This harks back to the modernisation theory that was so popular in the 1950s and 1960s. The outcome of many of these neoliberal interventions, however, has been devastating.

The purely technical and administrative thrust of the neoliberal PBSB approach lamentably neglected to diagnose and treat the root causes of the fragility and failure of those societies. Perhaps neoliberalism is not interested in looking for the root causes. The failure to understand the complicated problems that the societies faced led to further fragility and collapse. This is so because their problem is, by its very nature, political – that is, intimately connected with state- and nation-building. The state- and nation-building project is not included in neoliberal interventionism; thus by design the intervention is not intended to remedy the problem that it supposedly addresses.

The connection between peacebuilding and statebuilding in addressing the pathologies that afflicted those societies was, therefore, based on technical short-term thinking; some would call it ideological, rather than solid research analysis and prescription. Peacebuilding and statebuilding are based on two different premises. The first deals with bringing people together – with reconciliation, bridging differences, avoiding misunderstandings and misconceptions, building trust and confidence, etc. The second is concerned with building national institutions, creating a political culture, routinising and bureaucratising politics, allocating power that leads to winners and losers, etc. The popular progressive model – which deals with long-term societal construction and which prioritises domestic over external intervention – may be better equipped than the neoliberal model to create harmony between peacebuilding and statebuilding. The rationale behind this conception is statebuilding (SB) in the popular progressive model concerns fundamental foundation of societal construction. This societal construction, in turn, needs to address power relation and allocation, socio-economic equitable distribution, regional and mode of livelihood balance, identity and citizenship parity, etc. Once popular progressive SB addresses these issues, PB becomes easier to achieve.

References

Barnett, Michael. 2006. 'Building a Republican Peace: Stabilizing States after War', *International Security*, vol. 30, no. 4, pp. 87–112.

Call, Charles T. 2008a. 'Ending Wars, Building States', in Charles T. Call and Vanessa Wyeth (eds.), *Building States to Build Peace*. Boulder, CO and London: Lynne Rienner Publishers.

Call, Charles T. 2008b. 'Building States to Build Peace? A Critical Analysis', *Journal of Peace Building and Development*, vol. 4, no. 2, pp. 60–74.

Call, Charles T. and Wyeth, Vanessa (eds.). 2008. *Building States to Build Peace*. Boulder, CO and London: Lynne Rienner Publishers.

Christensen, Darin and Laitin, David D. 2019. *African States since Independence: Order, Development, and Democracy*. New Haven, CT and London: Yale University Press.

Curtis, Devon. 2012. 'The Contested Politics of Peace-Building in Africa', in Devon Curtis and Gwinyayi Dzinesa (eds.), *Peace-Building, Power, and Politics in Africa*. Athens: Ohio University Press.

Grävingholt, Järn, Gänzle, Stefan and Ziaja, Sebastian. 2009. 'Policy Brief: Concepts of Peace-Building and State Building – How Compatible Are They?' German Development Institute, 11 March.

Harrison, Graham. 2012. 'Financing Peace? The World Bank, Reconstruction, and Liberal Peace-Building', in Devon Curtis and Gwinyayi A. Dzinesa (eds.), *Peace-Building, Power, and Politics in Africa*. Athens: Ohio University Press.

Harrison, Graham. 2010. *Neoliberal Africa: The Impact of Global Social Engineering*. London and New York: Zed Books.

Heathershaw, John. 2013. 'Towards Better Theories of Peace-Building: Beyond the Liberal Peace Debate, Review Essay', *Peacebuilding*, vol. 1, no. 2, pp. 275–282.

Hyden, Goran. 2013. *African Politics in Comparative Perspective*, 2nd ed. New York: Cambridge University Press.

Kamrava, Mehran. 2000. *Politics and Society in the Developing World*. London and New York: Routledge.

Mac Ginty, Roger. 2008. 'Indigenous Peace-Making versus the Liberal Peace', *Cooperation and Conflict: Journal of the Nordic International Studies Association*, vol. 43, no. 2, pp. 139–163.

Mamdani, Mahmood. 1996. *Citizens and Subjects: Contemporary Africa and the Legacy of Late Colonialism*. Princeton, NJ: Princeton University Press.

Mazrui, Ali A. and Wiafe-Amoako, Francis. 2016. *African Institutions: Challenges to Political, Social, and Economic Foundations of Africa's Development*. Lanham, MD and London: Rowman and Littlefield.

OECD. 2010. OECD Report on Peacebuilding and Statebuilding.

Paris, Roland. 2002. 'International Peace-Building and the *Mission Civilisatrice*', *Review of International Studies*, vol. 28, no. 4, pp. 637–656.

Poggi, Gianfranco. 1978. *The Development of the Modern State*. London: Hutchinson.

Richmond, Oliver P. 2013. 'The Legacy of State Formation Theory for Peace-building and Statebuilding', *International Peacekeeping*, vol. 20, no. 3, pp. 299–315.

Robert, David. 2012. 'Saving Liberal Peace-Building from Itself', *Peace Review: A Journal of Social Justice*, vol. 24, pp. 366–373.

Schaar, John H. 2000. *Legitimacy in the Modern State*. New Brunswick, NJ and Oxford: Transaction Publishers.

Tom, Patrick. 2017. *Liberal Peace and Post-Conflict Peacebuilding in Africa*. London: Palgrave Macmillan.

Zaum, Dominik. 2012. 'Statebuilding and Governance: The Conundrum of Legitimacy and Local Ownership', in Devon Curtis and Gwinyayi Dzinesa (eds.), *Peace-Building, Power, and Politics in Africa*. Athens: Ohio University Press.

6 Conclusion
Summary and highlights

Introduction

This book has set out to examine two theoretical approaches to peace-building and statebuilding (PBSB) in Africa. These are neoliberal PBSB and popular progressive PBSB. Neoliberal PBSB primarily concerns conflict societies, and as such it aspires to repair post-conflict societies. Following the end of the Cold War, neoliberalism emerged as the dominant ideology. It thus embarked on unopposed world-wide interventionism, with the intention of refashioning non-Western societies in the image of Western norms and values (Harrison, 2010; Thiessen, 2011). Its dominance stems from the spread, acceptance and adoption it received worldwide. This endeavour was buttressed by the philosophy of globalism and universalism – a philosophy that, with its strong rhetoric and reorientation of a common humanity, increasingly gained primacy. The notion of a common humanity gained world-wide currency and appeal in the era of neoliberalism. This common humanity rhetoric, however, failed to encompass shared rights and responsibilities for all. The shared rights would include the right to shared use of global resources, thereby combating inequality and poverty. The billions of US dollars spent annually from our common global resources for weapons by wealthy and powerful states would have been used to alleviate the suffering of peoples in developing societies, the inequality, poverty and underdevelopment that underpin conflicts. That would indicate a genuine global humanity.

As a consequence, while certain nations emerged as net winners, others became losers, thereby rendering common humanity simply a trap for the weaker ones. In other words, neoliberalism-driven globalism and universalism further aggravated social inequality, economic deprivation and inequality within and among nations, leading to cultural and political xenophobia. Indeed, it simply reinforced the pyramidal hierarchy of inequality within and among nations. Perhaps its most visible negative repercussion was to be seen in the areas of peacebuilding and statebuilding in conflict societies.

Soon, therefore, neoliberal interventionist PBSB drew immense criticism from every direction (right and left) (cf. Fukuyama, 2007; Harrison, 2010; Paris, 1997; Richmond, 2006). In some circles, the growing realisation of neoliberalism's inability to adequately address the challenges of PBSB spurred the search for an alternative model – a search that is still stifled by the overbearing shadow of neoliberalism. One of the problems is predicated on neoliberalism's stubborn adherence to faulty and inadequate prescriptions and its tireless labouring to impose solutions that prevent other alternative solutions from being tested. Moreover, neoliberalism faces no serious challenge in academia or among policymakers, activists and civil society from the global south, particularly Africa. To the contrary, it is increasingly gaining terrain, albeit dressing different names. This has given it unchallenged global hegemonic status. For neoliberals, the failures they encounter can be explained as simply the inadequate passage of time and lack of proper implementation. The attitude is: if these shortcomings are remedied, neoliberalism will work; so let's give it time. Even those who are critical of the approach would not go beyond reform: reform rather than radical overhaul. This work, on the other hand, proposes a fundamental change both in our way of thinking and in our behaviour.

To do this, perhaps, the first step would be to acknowledge the social construction of knowledge and knowledge production, and the consequent construction of reality that underlie action. In this assumption, the social construction of reality produces a particular version of reality, a version of a particular cultural group. The cultural group's discourse on a particular version of reality and knowledge that deny prevalence of other social construction of reality and knowledge assumes universal and hegemonic position, and dictates its power. This particularistic version of reality and knowledge serves particular interests and creates division and inequality in society. Socially constructed discourses are mediated by power relations and privilege certain groups over others (Tanabe, 2017). It is this philosophical foundation of neoliberal PBSB that needs deconstruction.

As we have seen in this book, the approaches of the two models to PBSB are based on fundamentally diverging foundations and outlooks. The divergence in approach – which would lead to different outcomes – should certainly spur controversy as to which model is the correct one. However, the popular progressive model has not been put into practice, and even the theory has not yet been well developed.

But criticism of the neoliberal model is growing increasingly vocal. Informed by that criticism, this book has sought to advance an alternative to neoliberal PBSB. Its central argument is that popular progressive PBSB will bring lasting and functional PBSB. This argument stems from the contention that PBSB is, by its very nature, domestic: it craves domestic indigenous institutions, mechanisms, knowledge, expertise, dynamics, authorities, negotiations, compromises, bargaining and consensus among stakeholders, which is time-consuming work and a task that could not be shouldered by external intervention. Moreover, the popular progressive model goes beyond the technical and administrative solution of neoliberalism, because PBSB is political by its very nature. In addition, it deals with profound societal construction – in technical parlance, nation and state formation.

This concluding chapter seeks to recap on the central arguments of the book, and thereby to provide some highlights. The following section examines neoliberal PBSB; then there is a look at popular progressive PBSB. This is followed by examination of the consequences of neoliberal interventions. The final section provides some concluding remarks.

Neoliberal peacebuilding and statebuilding

Neoliberalism's real political breakthrough came in 1980, following the election of Ronald Reagan as president in the USA and Margaret Thatcher as prime minister in the UK (Kymlicka, 2017: 4). Reagan and Thatcher are credited with altering the course of world politics: the shift to the radical right (known as neoconservatism) had immense consequences for the world system, as well as for the welfare state system, particularly in the UK, and became the ideological imprint of the right. The US–UK version of neoliberalism was of a distinctive stripe, leading scholars to talk of Anglo-American or transatlantic neoliberalism (Jessop, n.d.). The duo's right-wing political ideology also found expression in an aggressive foreign policy that sought to reshape the world order. Their crusade against the Soviet Union and progressive forces in the developing world became increasingly and dangerously provocative, violent and destructive. This was seen in the number of conflicts around the world triggered by the direct and indirect machinations of the US and the UK. This was the peak of the Cold War where successive Western regimes were locked in an ideological struggle with the Eastern Bloc for world domination. Reagan's famous/infamous description of the Soviet Union as the 'Evil Empire' was neoliberalism's effort and fight against state socialism, and it paid off. Those two countries stood on the side of the apartheid system in South Africa; supported brutal regimes like that of Mobutu in Zaire; trained and armed the Mujahidin in Afghanistan; encouraged and armed right-wing movements in Latin America. The West – the USA, Britain and France, in particular – supported the fascist Salazar regime in Portugal against the quest for liberation in Mozambique, Angola and Guinea Bissau (cf. Schmidt, 2013, 2018). Ronald Reagan, for instance, expressed his support in an interview for the notorious apartheid system:

> Can we abandon a country that has stood by us in every war we've ever fought, a country that strategically is essential to the free world in its production of minerals we all must have and so forth? I just feel that ... if we're going to sit down at a table and negotiate with the Russians, surely we can keep the door open and continue to negotiate with a friendly nation like South Africa.
>
> (Schmidt, 2013: 110)

The axis of apartheid, fascism and neoliberalism devastated southern and central Africa. Reagan had no problem calling apartheid South Africa 'a friendly nation'.

Neoliberal interventionist PBSB gained world momentum and dominance in the wake of the Cold War. The demise of the Soviet Union and state socialism led to the rise of mono-polarity. The crowning of the USA as the sole superpower was declared to be the triumph of neoliberalism as the dominant and unchallenged world ideology, a manifestation of the 'end of history' (Fukuyama, 1992). It was also taken as confirmation of the superiority of the capitalist system of political economy. Resonating this, Ralf Dahrendorf (1990: 34) wrote,

> At the end of the century, however, we see the 'unabashed victory of economic and political liberalism'. Moreover, 'the triumph of the West, of the Western idea' marks 'the end of history as such' because there are no fundamental conflicts of concepts of order left. Instead we begin to see the outline of what Fukuyama insists on calling a 'universal homogenous [sic!] state' which consists of 'liberal democracy in the political sphere combined with easy access to VCR and stereos in the economic'.
>
> (Emphasis in original)

The post-Cold War post-Westphalia era saw the conflation or rather fusion of liberalism into neoliberalism, particularly in the area of

PBSB. The so-called liberal peacebuilding and statebuilding there-fore evolved into neoliberalism. Three distinct features characterise the fusion: (i) it, discursively and operationally, became hegemonic, shunning other strands as defective, (ii) it is highly intervention-ist and impositioning, (iii) it has an inclination towards moulding conflict-shattered societies along Western models. Classical liberalism that propagates individual freedom, equality, fraternity, diversity, plu-rality, recognition, self-fulfilment and realisation was replaced by ho-mogenisation, monopolisation, imposition, compulsion, intervention and domination. Post-Cold War PBSB, as policy as well as discourse became monolithic. Its genesis, in a normative frame, could be traced to the UN Peace Agenda framed in humanitarian interventionism. This created the prelude for multilateral and unilateral intervention whether in the form of UN authorised intervention or individual pow-erful Western states driven by geo-strategic interests.

This development in turn encouraged the followers of neoliberalism to prescribe a normative world order that would shape the entire world in the image of the West. In the neoliberal era, the only available con-sumable item on the market has been the Western model, and it has been hawked overtly and boldly. Some years ago, it might have been perceived to be imprudent and reprehensible to impose a Western model on non-Western developing societies. Most significantly, how-ever, now there is no world power that can hinder it. The road is now wide open for the Western big powers to dictate their model by persua-sion or coercion. To many, this behaviour by the Western great powers smacks of a return to colonial behaviour, a sort of neo-colonialism or neo-imperialism (Shittu, 2015).

The unfettered prescription and imposition of the neoliberal solu-tion has been clearly visible in none other than PBSB. Western powers, with great ease and arbitrariness, have sought to reconstruct states and rebuild peace in conflict-afflicted fragile societies and collapsed states. Societies whose states have collapsed or are dysfunctional are dubbed a danger to themselves and the wider world. Therefore, it is perceived that the 'international community' – a euphemism for the Western powers – has a responsibility to reconstruct states and re-build peace for them. Some, even claim that Western powers first cre-ate crisis and failure of those societies in order to latter reconstruct them. This could happen with direct Western intervention or through a "friendly" state, for instance, Ethiopia's invasion of Somalia in 2006. More often than not, however, this Western intervention has made the situation worse. This underpins the growing criticism that is levelled at neoliberal PBSB. The criticism pivots around the main concern that neoliberal peacebuilding is primarily imposed from outside, is technical, managerial and short term, and thus is not intended to address the root causes. It is also concerned with the post-war external reconstruction of societies. It is, perhaps, the short-term approach that explains the administrative and technical strategy of the neoliberal solution. As this book has demonstrated, by its very nature, statebuilding is political, and politics is about power allocation; who takes what, when and how. Politics produces winners and losers; and that in turn engenders conflict, as the losers may resort to alternative means of addressing their grievances. The central focus of neoliberalism is aptly depicted thus:

> the neoliberal world does not purport so much to describe the world as it is, but the world as it should be. The point of neoliberalism is not to make a model that is more adequate to the real world, but to make the real world more adequate to its model. This is not merely an intellectual fantasy, it is a very real political project, to realise which neoliberalism has conquered the commanding heights of global intellectual, political and economic power, all of which are mobilised to realise the neoliberal project of subjecting the whole world's population to the judgement and morality of capitalism.
>
> (Clarke, 2005: 57)

Indeed, neoliberalism's theoretical and conceptual mission is not to find a model that fits the situation of conflict and post-conflict societies, but to fit those societies to that model. The reconfiguration of developing societies along Western lines became neoliberalism's preoccupation. A preoccupation that spurs blatant intervention defines contemporary world order. As a reflection of this, President Donald Trump, on a visit to Poland, in July 2017, in a speech he delivered stated that they will do everything to preserve the West's way of life and civilisation.

The highly normative approach of neoliberalism, bent as it is on reconfiguring the world in its own image, instead of adjusting the world's image according to reality, renders externally imposed PBSB highly dysfunctional and at best short-lived. It might achieve a ceasefire and the temporary cessation of hostilities by combatants. But since peace is not merely the absence of war, neoliberal intervention could not provide the necessary ingredients for positive peace, which is also a prerequisite for statebuilding. The provisions of positive peace pertain to economic, social, cultural, political and structural issues and foundations. Unless, these foundations are adequately laid down, any cessation of hostilities will not proceed to enduring peace. One of the shortcomings of externally driven peacebuilding – not to mention statebuilding – is the factor of the time frame and the availability of resources. In terms of the time frame, external actors are constrained by short-termism: they plan for just a few years. They cannot and do not plan to stay indefinitely, which is what peacebuilding would require (cf. Brahimi, 2007). In terms of the availability of resources, externally driven peacebuilding also suffers a shortage. External peacebuilding is resource intensive, because it is highly dependent on external personnel, experts, advisors, weapons and instruments. These are always in short supply. Another fault-line is the primary focus on combatants. Any externally mediated cessation of hostilities is concerned with stopping the war; thus it deals with the warring parties. But this prioritisation of the warring parties occurs at the expense of many other stakeholders. The perception is that to include all stakeholders would take too much time, consume too many resources, complicate the agenda, affect venue selection, etc. In short, a host of problems would have to be dealt with; and that would make resolving the conflict highly problematic, if not impossible. Those excluded stakeholders whose interests are not taken on board would inevitably cast around for their own alternative mechanisms, which would – sooner or later – lead to further conflict. All this contributes to the delegitimisation of the neoliberal peacebuilding process (Thiessen, 2011).

With regard to statebuilding, the interventionists are not even concerned with statebuilding – and indeed their actions may lead to state destruction. Condoleezza Rice, secretary of state in George W. Bush's administration, was candid enough to admit that the USA had no plans for introducing democracy or for rebuilding the Iraqi state after they had deposed Saddam Hussein: 'Now, we didn't go to Iraq to bring democracy to the Iraqis. And I try in the book to really explain that that wasn't the purpose' (ABC News, 2011). This says a lot about neoliberal intervention: it is ready to destroy, but has no interest whatsoever in subsequent rebuilding. The security concern that induced the USA to invade Iraq in 2003 was the geostrategic interest of the United States (Thiessen, 2011). It becomes evident from Rice's response that it was not the security of the people of Iraq that necessitated war. It is clear from what happened in the aftermath of the war that the invaders failed to repair the house they had destroyed: that would be too expensive, too time- and resource-consuming, and therefore should be left to the Iraqis. The same could be said of NATO's invasion of Libya. The NATO countries were willing to destroy the Libyan state, but were not willing to engage in post-Gaddafi SBPB. Both societies collapsed following the neoliberal intervention, exposing the societies to Al Qaeda, Islamic State (ISIS) and other extremist groups. A state that was supposed to provide security, stability, peace and protection to its citizens was erased by neoliberal intervention, leaving the space wide open to extremist groups.

Statebuilding is much more demanding than peacebuilding. Statebuilding is quintessentially institution-building. Some of the fundamental institutions of state – such as the legislature, executive and judiciary, as well as national and local economic, social and cultural institutions – need to be put in place in order for a properly functioning, representative and democratic state to evolve. Institution building is not only setting the skeletons. The flesh that covers the skeleton also needs to be constructed. The flesh includes human power, political culture, moral, ethos and behaviours. Certainly, this requires time, energy, popular participation, ownership and equitable distribution of resources and capacities. Above all, it needs routinisation, predictability, transparency and accountability: in sum, a conversion into culture. In the final analysis, the point is to build a state that all citizens feel belongs to them. They need to feel that they own it and are prepared to live together in it. For this to happen, they have to build it themselves. Clearly, this cannot be achieved by visitors: it is a task that can only be fulfilled by the occupants of the house. All members of the household need to participate, and not – as is the case with neoliberalism – just a few select members. This process could take decades, if not generations.

The popular progressive peacebuilding and statebuilding model

The inappropriateness of the neoliberal model of PBSB in developing societies in general, and Africa in particular, prompts us to look for an alternative model. In this book I have suggested an alternative model that I call popular progressive PBSB. As this book has tried to demonstrate, popular progressive PBSB is superior to neoliberal PBSB for a number of reasons. First, PBSB is, by its very nature, domestic and goes beyond post-conflict reconstruction. Conflict is produced, in the first place, because of fragility of society. This cannot be tackled by a neoliberal interventionist approach. It concerns profound societal construction, and so involves a long and gradual transformation. Second, it utilises domestic resources and infrastructure – such as cultural, social, historical, structural and institutional; indigenous authorities, knowledge, wisdom, expertise, mechanisms, etc. – that are arguably the domain of the popular progressive model. Third, society-building – in technical parlance, nation and state formation – is work enough for several generations and is a process that defies any quick, neoliberal fix. According to the general literature (cf. Gellner, 1983; Smith, 1986), the conflation of state formation and nation formation as a protracted process exemplifies a simultaneous dual process of integration and separation. Here, it is of significance to acknowledge the difference of mechanism between mono-ethnic nation and multi-ethnic nation (while the former is based on cultural identity, the latter is based on territoriality).

Integration and cohesion stand for the notion of the nation-state, in the sense that a state should fit a particular nation, and a nation should be represented by its own state; meanwhile separation denotes delimitation between two entities that are dialectically interwoven, yet analytically separable. This separability denotes the contours of state–society relations that define and reflect constitutive modernity. Notions of pacification and emancipation appropriately describe the process of integration and separation. The organic processes of integration and separation as the evolution of nation- and statebuilding in Africa, for instance, were continuously disrupted in history. This disruption was also a disruption of the organic domestic process of peacebuilding, as conceptualised by popular progressive peacebuilding. Colonialism represented a first historical in the continuum of disruption of the evolution of the integration of nation and state in Africa. A second and a third disruption followed, in the form of the neo-colonial/Cold War period, and the global war on terror followed by the scramble for resources. These disruptions may have differed in form, but not in content. The disruption denotes, on the one hand, the absence of state penetration, since the colonial state was an alien entity, representing a different, cosmopolitan nation; on the other hand, it corrupted and compromised the statebuilding process by alienating from its societal foundation. Even the post-colonial state (which was supposed to restore the state–society relationship to its natural place and process) simply continued – albeit perhaps in a different form – the alienated and conflictual state–society relationship. This is because the post-colonial continuation connoted a deeply misconfigured and corrupted structure and relationship.

In the post-colonial era, serious and concerted endeavours took place to remedy the deeply misconfigured and corrupted structure and relationship. Nevertheless, the endeavour faced another disruption – neo-colonialism, which was succeeded by post-Cold War neoliberal intervention. What I term here the second historical disruption – the neo-colonial/Cold War disruption –constituted an impediment to the rehabilitation and restoration of political, cultural, economic, national institutions and of the dignity and identity of Africans. The physical dislocation of colonialism was not accompanied by either economic or cultural dislocation. The mischiefs of erstwhile colonial masters was cogently described thus,

> Without a qualm it dispenses with its flags, and even with certain of its more hated expatriate officials. This means, so it claims, that it is 'giving' independence to its former subjects, to be followed by 'aid' for their development. Under cover of such phrases, however, it devises innumerable ways to accomplish objectives formerly achieved by naked colonialism. It is this sum total of these modern attempts to perpetuate colonialism while at the same time talking about 'freedom', which has come to be known as *neo-colonialism*.
>
> (Nkrumah, 1970: 239)

This manifests itself most vividly in the Francophone world, where France's iron grip on its colonies of yesterday is still very real. This even casts a long shadow over the African Union's recently inaugurated and highly celebrated Continental Free Trade Area initiative.

The economic and cultural dominance of yesterday's master has precluded full liberation, which would have opened the way to the implementation of popular progressive strategies, programmes and projects of peacebuilding, statebuilding and development. This in turn has fractured societies, leading to conflict, war and fragility. Neoliberalism has exploited this and has embarked on the social engineering of those societies in line with Western norms and values – a continuation of the colonial project, though in a slightly different format. It has not remedied the problem, however. The project of peacebuilding in its fundamental and dialectical sense is a project of development. As Boutros-Ghali noted in his *Agenda for Peace*, 'There is no development nor democracy without peace ... And without development, the basis for democracy is lacking and societies will relapse into violence' (United Nations, 1992: 43). Therefore, peacebuilding, as John Paul Lederach (1999) notes, entails everything that conceptualises, produces and upholds the wide variety of necessary stages and approaches in order to transform conflict situation into pacific and durable relations. But this could not be achieved by neoliberalism.

In light of this, it is argued, only popular progressive peacebuilding is capable of bringing sustainable and functional peace. Peace as a requirement of statebuilding – and vice versa – could only be achieved in the popular progressive model. It would also strengthen the process of statebuilding. The protracted evolutionary processes, dynamics and mechanisms of nation and state formation that are founded on the idiosyncratic specificities of the particular society that the popular progressive approach embraces will ensure sustainable, functional and permanent comprehensive peace. This is so because the process is the outcome of protracted negotiation, bargaining, compromise and representation of societal groups, which serves to foster agency and ownership, and to inculcate a will to live together. The will to live together is generated subsequent to elaborate and protracted interaction leading to trust and confidence. This, in turn, rests on the construction of domestic institutions and structures; economic, social and political transformations and ethnolinguistic harmony, cohesion, social equitability. These were previously relegated by colonialism to informality, and then ignored or denied by neoliberalism. Neoliberalism as a hegemonic ideology strives to create uniformity.

In multi-ethnic societies, fostering the will to live together among citizens is of great significance for sustainable and functional peace and successful peacebuilding. The will to live together results from the harmonisation of the processes and mechanisms of state and nation formation (Bereketeab, 2007). Moreover, it is the outcome of historical, cultural, political and institutional accumulations over generations. Ultimately, this will foster genuine social contract between society and state, and legitimacy of the state, which is the mainstay of peace and peacebuilding:

> The legitimacy parameter refers to the extent to which a state commands public loyalty to the governing regime, and the extent to which domestic support is generated for that government's legislation and policy. Such support must be created through a voluntary and reciprocal arrangement of effective governance and citizenship founded upon broadly accepted principles of government selection and succession that is recognized both locally and internationally. States in which the ruling regime lacks either broad and voluntary domestic support or general international recognition suffer a lack of legitimacy.
>
> (Carment and Samy, 2014: 7)

The reciprocal arrangement of effective governance and citizenship rests on the cardinal principle of state–society relations, where the state delivers services to society, while society concomitantly confers legitimacy on the state. Moreover, the manner through which the state came into being, particularly the ruling regime, also duly determines the internality and externality sources of legitimacy. A popularly constructed state would have a high likelihood of legitimacy and engendering sustainable SBPB.

The evolution of societal pacification and state emancipation as embedded in the popular progressive model would engender social and political equilibrium, in the sense of harmony between state and society that, in the long run, is predicated on the bestowal of the internality and externality of legitimacy. The coexistence and mutual enhancement of state emancipation and societal pacification that reflect advanced level of nation and state formation would contribute to world peace, security and development.

Social contract among citizens, as well as between state and society, can only emanate from internality – an internality that not only acknowledges and celebrates, but is also contingent upon, idiosyncrasies, contexts, specificities and realities. Its maturity is also highly contingent on time and place: that is, it needs time and has to be based on the specificities of a particular place. History teaches us that development in Europe took several hundred years, and moreover was internally guided and dictated. This means it took time as well as was based on the specificities of European reality. That historical experience does not lend convincing evidence for the success of externality. Additionally, externality is selective. In its selectivity, it promotes some groups while demoting others. Externality that raises one group above another is thus antithetical to a social contract that defines legitimacy. In this sense, externality would generate disharmony and fissures that would adversely affect legitimation. Externality looks outward rather than inward. It is therefore proposed

> that peacebuilding actors not work from universal blueprints, but engage in caring and empathetic multilevel consultation in order to provide the grassroots with a voice, operate on the norms they are trying to instil (e.g., democracy, equality, social justice), and place local community concerns before liberal/neoliberal goals. Thus, peacebuilding actors are required to conduct continual critique of their activities, be well aware of their 'baggage' they bring to peace activities, and work as 'enablers for localized dynamics of peace' at the grassroots level of society.
>
> (Thiessen, 2011: 118)

It is not lack of 'critique of their activities' or absence of awareness 'of their baggage', although it may also be the case, which is the problem, but the receptiveness of the reality on the ground of those activities and baggage that we should be concerned with.

The challenges the popular progressive model faces are the pervasiveness and dominance that the neoliberal model has built up in recent years. It has grown so pervasive and so dominant that it is blindly accepted everywhere and by everyone. It has even captured a substantial section of the African elites, scholars and civil society organisations. Its doctrine of universalism, globalism and common humanity is uncritically swallowed whole. In this regard, a crucial question is the extent to which the popular progressive model could unseat the neoliberal approach to gain a dominant position in developing societies. Its crowning is vital for the sustainability and functioning PBSB.

Consequences of neoliberal interventions

In the past couple of decades, we have seen several blatant interventions by bigger and powerful states in internal affairs of usually conflict-ridden, fragile and weak states. It seems, it is the weakness or inability of the object state to defend itself that induces the intervention. This perhaps resonates the logic of might is right. Once intervention in the internal affairs of sovereign states became fashionable – in violation of the Westphalian international regime – world security and stability deteriorated considerably. The Westphalian non-interference regime guided the international state system. The gradual undermining of the Westphalian system – which held sway for almost four centuries – without putting a solid replacement in its place, has subjected the international system to considerable peril. What makes it so dangerous is that there are no clear principles, guidelines, rules or morals for why the intervention takes place, who intervenes, to what end and for how long. The UN Security Council – the international organ that is mandated to approve intervention – is often overridden by powerful states. This undermining of the UNSC in exercising its mandates as an ultimate authority that deals with world peace and security is dangerous and paralyses it to the extent it is not able to have consensus on some important issues such as the Syrian and Yemeni crisis. This puts the notion of international community as a world body in a precarious position. In addition, and perhaps more serious, are the consequences to target societies. One could easily be led to infer that the consequences of the intervention for the target society are not properly considered. In fact, intervention goes ahead even if all the indications are that it could aggravate the problem. Indeed, it seems to be guided by the Machiavellian doctrine of 'the end justifies the means'. The end is to create neoliberal democratic societies, and that should be carried through whatever the price. It is also unidirectional, from north to south, but never the opposite. How would the north react if interventionism is initiated from the south?

Generally, under the Westphalian system, the behaviour of states towards one another was predictable. Quite often, big powers are constrained not to violate rights of small state, and they have to respect their integrity, unity, peace and security. If there prevails a compelling reason, it has to be done in a predictable, transparent and accountable manner, but also through multilateralism that upholds international laws and conventions. But the predictability vanished as soon as the Westphalian regime receded and a new and unknown terrain was introduced. This unknown terrain in international state relations is marked by the right of powerful states. The rule of the powerful is now characterised by two features: interventionist PBSB and forcible regime change in states deemed to be in breach of good conduct. Furthermore, this is done in the guise of humanitarianism and following the principle of responsibility to protect (R2P). This development was facilitated by the end of the Cold War and the triumph of the hegemonic neoliberal world order, whose concrete empirical manifestation was further consolidated by the 9/11 terrorist attacks on the USA (Schmidt, 2018). Following those heinous attacks, the White House launched what it called its 'global war on terror' (GWT).

The GWT was distinguished by two features that came to be known as the Bush Doctrine: (i) pre-emptive action and (ii) regime change. Pre-emptive action is guided by the philosophy of taking action before an alleged enemy strikes. This gives the USA the right to attack any government, in any corner of the world that is suspected of harbouring ill-wishes against the USA or its allies and interests around the world. The second doctrine, regime change, is concerned with getting rid of regimes that are believed to fall short of neoliberal values and norms. Perhaps a third element could be added to the post-Westphalian rights of the powerful: the danger of fragility and collapse of states. Societies with fragile and collapsed states are considered a danger to themselves and to the international community; therefore, it is the duty of big powers to construct a state for them. This responsibility is to be shouldered by the international community – a concept that has now generally been discredited with regard to PBSB: in reality, the international community means the West.

These three aspects of the Bush Doctrine laid the foundation for neoliberal intervention in Afghanistan, Iraq, Somalia, South Sudan, Libya, Mali, Syria, DRC, etc. The outcome for these societies has been devastating. Some of the states that have been destroyed by regime-change neoliberal interventions had strong, well-established welfare systems. Under Gaddafi, for instance, Libya had the highest living standards in Africa. Once the Libyan state was destroyed by the NATO invasion, all the socio-economic security that the Libyans had was gone. In addition, Libya became a lawless chaotic territory run by bandits and warlords, where every sort of crime was common. The neoliberal interventions induced radicalism, fundamentalism, extremism and terrorism. The emergence of radical extremist groups such as the Al Qaeda – in all its different versions, Al Shebab, ISIS and others – is directly related to the policies of regime change. The devastating consequences of the interventions for the people of Afghanistan, Iraq, Somalia, Yemen, Libya and Syria are really difficult to comprehend. Beyond these societies, the consequences also afflict vulnerable societies in Africa and Asia, as well as the West.

Conclusion

This concluding chapter has sought to recap on some of the messages that the book has tried to convey, and to provide some highlights. The book is an exposition of two models of PBSB: the neoliberal and the popular progressive ones. This book, while critically appraising the suitability of neoliberalism as a model of PBSB in developing societies, has tried to demonstrate the superiority of the popular progressive model. The core difference between the two models is succinctly presented as follows. The neoliberal model is an imposition of the now dominant Western ideology (some call it social engineering) to configure conflict-ridden non-Western societies on the basis of Western values and norms. It is primarily a technical, administrative and short-term solution. The alternative to this is the popular progressive model, which is concerned with the fundamentals of the constitution of society, both nation formation and state formation, as requirements for enduring PBSB. Being primarily domestic, the popular progressive model would utilise indigenous infrastructures, institutions, mechanisms, authorities and capacities. It is liberating and empowering of all citizens, as it endows them with the ownership of their own destiny and agency.

As this book goes to show, in essence, the two models could be said to represent two diametrically opposed models – not only as models of PBSB, but more profoundly as models for societal construction – or put another way, for nation and state formation. The overarching problem facing Africa has to do with the basics of statebuilding and nation-building. Modern state- and nation-building in Africa was crafted, designed, steered and implemented by colonialism, without any participation by or consultation with Africans, according to the metropolitan architecture. The first concomitant pathology of this metropolitan architecture was the creation of hostile spheres, in the form of rural and urban. Since the urban sphere was intended to be configured in the image of the metropolitan power, its relations with the rural sphere were inimical. That animosity continued even after the European masters had left. The post-colonial state found it difficult to liberate itself from the colonial legacy. The perpetuation of the metropolitan architecture thus kept state and society apart in the post-colonial context, too. These two entities often treated one another as enemies. Colonialism was succeeded by neo-colonialism, the Cold War, the war on terror and the scramble for resources. These all perpetuated external intervention, which denied Africa the opportunity to map out its own routes, make its own mistakes, and pursue its own visions and aspirations. It undermined statebuilding and nation-building as societal construction. Intervention produced societies that ended up fragile – or even collapsing – as the upshot of the failure of state- and nation-building. Those societies also encountered another externally driven experiment: neoliberal interventionist PBSB. The consequences of the neoliberal intervention to subjugate societies and the larger world are colossal: the 2015 world refugee crisis is only one epitome. All this constitutes the epicentre of the pathologies bedevilling post-colonial states and societies. Resolving the problems means dealing with the epicentre. The magnitude of the epicentre demands radical and innovative models, approaches, agencies, structures, mechanisms and institutions. This may require theoretical, conceptual and methodological reorientation, as well as gearing different praxis. The objective of the popular progressive model, as advocated in this book, is thus to use these radical and innovative instruments to remedy the cleavage that exists between state and society – something that is of the utmost necessity for sustainable PBSB. The popular progressive alternative to the neoliberal model would undo all that colonialism did and that the post-colonial state failed to address. Most importantly, it would map, scope, design, strategise, synergise and synthesise an alternative to neoliberalism that is capable of earning popularity and legitimacy. The epistemology and ontology that underpin neoliberal peacebuilding and statebuilding and popular progressive peacebuilding and statebuilding have completely different pedigrees. Finally, this book could be seen as critique of the neoliberal interventionist attempt at reconfiguring developing societies along the Western mould.

References

ABC News. 2011. 'Condoleezza Rice's Retrospect on Iraq: We Could Have Done Better', by George Stephanopoulos, 2 November. https://abcnews. go.com/blogs/politics/2011/11/condoleezza-reces-retrospect. Accessed on 11 June 2019.

Bereketeab, Redie. 2007. *Eritrea: The Making of a Nation, 1890–1991.* Trenton, NJ and Asmara: The Red Sea Press.

Brahimi, Lakhdar. 2007. 'State Building in Crisis and Post-Conflict Countries', presented at 7th Global Forum on Reinventing Government, Building Trust in Government, 26–29 June, Vienna, Austria.

Carment, David and Samy, Yiagadeesen. 2014. 'The Future of War: Understanding Fragile States and What to Do about Them', in Ingo Trauschweizer and Steven M. Miner (eds.), *Failed States and Fragile Societies: A New World Order?* Athens: Ohio University Press, pp. 3–27.

Clarke, Simon. 2005. 'The Neoliberal Theory of Society', in Alfredo Saad-Filho and Deborah Johnston (eds.), *Neoliberalism: A Critical Reader.* London: Pluto Press, pp. 50–59.

Dahrendorf, Ralf. 1990. *Reflections on the Revolution in Europe.* London: Chatto & Windus.

Fukuyama, Francis. 2007. 'Liberalism versus Statebuilding', *Journal of Democracy*, vol. 18, no. 3, pp. 10–13.

Fukuyama, Francis. 1992. *The End of History and the Last Man.* New York: Avon Books.

Gellner, Ernest. 1983. *Nations and Nationalism.* Oxford and Cambridge, MA: Blackwell Publishers.

Harrison, Graham. 2010. *Neoliberal Africa: The Impact of Global Social Engineering.* London and New York: Zed Books.

Jessop, Bob. n.d. 'From Thatcherism to New Labour: Neo-Liberalism, Workfarism, and Labour Market Regulation', published by the Department of Sociology, Lancaster University at: http://www.comp.lancs.ac.uk/sociology/soc131rj.pdf. Accessed on 25 June 2019.

Kymlicka, Will. 2017. 'Multiculturalism without Citizenship?' in Anna Triandafyllidou (ed.), *Multicultural Governance in a Mobile World.* Edinburgh: Edinburgh University Press, pp. 139–161.

Lederach, John Paul. 1999. *Sustainable Reconciliation in Divided Societies.* Washington, DC: United States Institute of Peace Press.

Nkrumah, Kwame. 1970. *Neo-Colonialism: The Last Stage of Imperialism.* London: PANAF.

Paris, Roland. 1997. 'Peace-Building and the Limits of Liberal Internationalism', *International Security*, vol. 22, no. 2, pp. 54–89.

Richmond, Oliver P. 2006. 'The Problem of Peace: Understanding the "Liberal Peace"', *Conflict, Security and Development*, vol. 6, no. 3, pp. 291–314.

Schmidt, Elizabeth. 2018. *Foreign Intervention in Africa after the Cold War: Sovereignty, Responsibility, and the War on Terror.* Athens: Ohio University Press.

Schmidt, Elizabeth. 2013. *Foreign Intervention in Africa: From the Cold War to the War on Terror.* Cambridge: Cambridge University Press.

Shittu, Raji. 2015. 'Africa and the Philosophy of the New Partnership for Africa's Development (NEPAD)', *Journal of African Foreign Affairs*, vol. 2, nos. 1–2, pp. 27–48.

Smith, Anthony D. 1986. *The Ethnic Origins of Nations.* Oxford and Cambridge, MA: Blackwell.

Tanabe, Juichiro. 2017. 'Beyond Liberal Peacebuilding: A Critique of Liberal Peacebuilding and Exploring a Modern Post-Liberal Hybrid Model of Peacebuilding', *International Relations and Diplomacy*, vol. 5, no. 8, pp. 447–459.

Thiessen, Charles. 2011. 'Emancipatory Peace-Building: Critical Response to (Neo)Liberal Trends', in Thomas Matyok, Jessica Senehi and Sean Byrne (eds.), *Critical Issues in Peace and Conflict Studies: Theory, Practice, and Pedagogy.* Lanham, MD and Plymouth: Lexington Books, pp. 115–140.

United Nations. 1992. *An Agenda for Peace: Preventive Diplomacy, Peacemaking and Peacekeeping,* Report of the Secretary General, A/47/277-5/24111, 17 June. New York: United Nations.

Index

For Product Safety Concerns and Information please contact our EU
representative GPSR@taylorandfrancis.com
Taylor & Francis Verlag GmbH, Kaufingerstraße 24, 80331 München, Germany

www.ingramcontent.com/pod-product-compliance
Lightning Source LLC
Chambersburg PA
CBHW050532270326
41926CB00015B/3187

* 9 7 8 0 3 6 7 5 5 8 9 6 3 *